MARCO POLO

CUBA

with Local Tips
*The author's special recommendations are
highlighted in yellow throughout this guide*

There are five symbols to help you find your way around this guide:

Marco Polo's top recommendations – the best in each category

sites with a scenic view

where the local people meet

where young people get together

(100/A1)
pages and coordinates for the road atlas
(U/A1) *coordinates for the city map of Havana inside back flap*
(O) *outside area covered by the city map*

MARCO ⊕ POLO

Travel guides and language guides in this series:

Algarve • Amsterdam • Australia • Berlin • Brittany • California
Channel Islands • Costa Brava/Barcelona • Costa del Sol/Granada
Côte d'Azur • Crete • Cuba • Cyprus • Eastern USA • Florence • Florida
Gran Canaria • Greek Islands/Aegean • Ibiza • Ireland • Istanbul • Lanzarote
London • Mallorca • Malta • New York • New Zealand • Normandy • Paris
Prague • Rhodes • Rome • Scotland • South Africa • Southwestern USA
Tenerife • Turkish Coast • Tuscany • Venice • Western Canada

French • German • Italian • Spanish

*Marco Polo would be very interested to hear your
comments and suggestions. Please write to:*

North America:
Marco Polo North America
70 Bloor Street East
Oshawa, Ontario, Canada
(B) 905-436-2525

United Kingdom:
World Leisure Marketing Ltd
Marco Polo Guides
Newmarket Drive
Derby DE24 8NW

*Our authors have done their research very carefully, but should any errors or omissions
have occurred, the publisher cannot be held responsible for any injury, damage
or inconvenience suffered due to incorrect information in this guide*

*Cover photograph: Salsa dancer (Mauritius: Cupak)
Photographs: Author (26); Eckenroth (84); Froese (28); HB Verlag Hamburg (12, 49);
Ihlow (25, 30, 33, 41, 43, 60, 66, 72, 77, 81); Lade: Bergmann (22), Ihlow (57),
Meissner (34), Walter (4), Welsh (58); Mauritius: Cupak (20), Gierth (69), Hayes (52),
Hubatka (99); Murillo (38); Spierenburg (28);
Timmermann (6, 11); White Star: Steinert (17)*

*2nd revised edition 1999
© Mairs Geographischer Verlag, Ostfildern, Germany
Author: Gesine Froese
Translation: Paul Fletcher
English edition 1999: Gaia Text
Editorial director: Ferdinand Ranft
Chief editor: Marion Zorn
Cartography Road Atlas: © Mairs Geographischer Verlag
Design and layout: Thienhaus/Wippermann
Printed in Germany*

CONTENTS

Discover Cuba

A new revolution has begun as Cuba's coral beaches and colonial towns welcome tourists with open arms

The building worker in Varadero looks on in surprise as a woman, clearly a tourist, walks past in the sweltering heat in bare feet. We chat for a few minutes, while he peels an orange. As he tells me about the new hotel they are building, he passes me a piece of the juicy fruit. I express my gratitude, but decline, remembering the poverty and feeling guilty of my privileged position as a tourist. But the man insists, almost insulted: 'Take it! We are all human.'

In Havana, as I walk down the Calle del Obispo towards the harbour, admiring the crumbling colonial buildings and brightly coloured old chevrolets, I am approached by an endless stream of curious locals. 'Where are you from? You speak English? Italian? Spanish?' By the time I reach the end of the street, I have been offered countless private restaurants, rooms, taxis, and boxes of cigars, and am exhausted by the effort of polite refusal.

The pleasures of the Caribbean: palm trees, surf and white sand at the Playa del Este east of Havana

In Santiago de Cuba, a 15-year-old girl tugs at my sleeve and looks at me pleadingly with her huge, dark eyes. She is wearing a short, tight skirt made from cheap, badly creased cotton, ringed with frills. She wants to come with me into my hotel. A mere child already out on the streets in search of a fast buck.

On the journey to Matanzas I find myself sitting next to Víctor. He would be happy to show me round the town, he says enthusiastically. He explains how petrol is in short supply, no buses are running and he has not seen the rest of his family for a week. He then tells me about his meagre monthly salary of around 200 pesos, which he exchanges on the black market for between 8 and 10 dollars, although he can increase this income quite considerably with tips earned from showing tourists round. 'You cannot do anything without dollars these days,' he explains. 'Last month we had to sell our old shoes. You have no idea how hard it is to bring up our children.' He invites me to his home, where he lives with his brother, sister-in-law and wife in a house owned by his father, who now lives in Havana. On a lace-covered chest of drawers stands a picture of the Virgin Mary, beside that of an Afro-Cuban deity carved out of wood. 'We have two altars in the house,' he remarks proudly as he turns down the volume on his Japanese stereo system, a present from relatives in Miami. All the while, Víctor's five-year-old son remains on his father's lap, holding on tightly.

On an excursion to Pinar del Río, every few kilometres we pass perilously close to a villager as he stands in the middle of the road offering hunks of cheese and other home-grown produce to the occasional passing traffic. All along the way small black vultures can be seen hovering in the sky above. Our driver, Luis, ejects his salsa cassette and puts on *Hotel California* by the Eagles, perhaps for the benefit of his European passengers. I haven't the heart to tell him I was enjoying the Cuban rhythms much more. We pass bridges, under which crowds of people gather in the shade. A little further on, a group of peasants are piling onto a huge sugar cane transporter, laughing and joking as they clamber on board.

Near Pinar del Río we visit a hotel that has recently opened. Everything is spick and span, but

The Valle de Viñales, tobacco-growing country beneath the strangely shaped limestone 'mogotes'

In the Marco Polo Spirit

Marco Polo was the first true world traveller. He travelled with peaceful intentions forging links between the East and the West. His aim was to discover the world, and explore different cultures and environments without changing or disrupting them. He is an excellent role model for the 20th-century traveller. Wherever we travel we should show respect for other peoples and the natural world.

WWF

there are hardly any guests. The view over the Viñales valley with its strange round-topped mounds is spectacular, and the manager enthuses optimistically about the great natural beauty of the region urging us to go riding or bird-watching, explore the caves and try a Cuban cocktail or two...'

Sketches of a Caribbean island. Anyone who has been to Cuba will relate instantly to these travel impressions. By the end of your holiday you will have plenty of similar stories to tell about this wonderful country, which can be both fascinating and infuriating, but never dull. Tourism is growing fast with the inevitable effects on a people who have been largely cut off from the capitalist West for over thirty years. The land of Fidel Castro, Che Guevara, Camilo Cienfuegos, and many other socialist heroes, is in the throes of a new revolution. But this time it is a gentle revolution, which is gradually moving Cuba towards capitalism. The collapse of the Eastern bloc and a trade embargo vigorously implemented by the USA brought on a desperate crisis in Cuba in 1994, but new trading partners in Canada, South America and Europe are helping to bring new hope to a country that has been shunned by much of the world for decades.

The Cuban government is introducing change cautiously. It began with some incisive reforms, billed by the foreign press as an 'economic revolution'. The Cuban peso, the value of which dropped to virtually nothing during the 'dollarization' of the economy, was revalued when the government ended the total ban on private markets. Cubans are now able to buy certain consumer goods with pesos. It was also decided that the generous social security system needed to be restructured. With the imposition of income tax and property tax, the first steps were taken towards the creation of a social market economy. These new laws mainly affect those who have set up a private enterprise and thus earn considerably more than state workers who have still not been given any pay increases, though the upward revaluation of the peso has eased their situation somewhat. With taxes levied on non-essentials, such as alcohol and tobacco, government finances have started to recover. It is beginning to look as though Cuba may well be able to achieve what few believed to be possible: a peaceful resolution to an acute crisis.

HISTORY AT A GLANCE

8000-2000 BC
Primitive tools made from stone, wood and shells point to the existence of cave-dwelling hunter-gatherers

1000 BC- AD 1000
An aboriginal group known as the Siboneys settle on the island, followed by the Taino Arawaks

27 October 1492
On the 16th day of his first voyage to the Americas, Christopher Columbus drops anchor in Bariay Bay

1512
Diego Velázquez founds Baracoa, Cuba's first town

1519
Hernán Cortés leads a fleet of ships from Cuba to Mexico

1522
The first African slaves arrive

From 1530
Havana's harbour becomes the 'Gateway to the New World' and a meeting point for vessels from other Spanish colonies involved in the silver trade

1604
The island's capital is moved to Santiago de Cuba

1720
The Spanish crown establishes a monopoly in the trade of tobacco and sugar. Small landowners rebel

1762
The English navy captures Havana, but later exchanges it for Spanish Florida

From 1789
The sugar trade flourishes as 30,000 prosperous French farmers flee to Cuba from the black revolution in Haiti

1820
Cuba is the world's biggest sugar exporter

1868
War of Independence under the leadership of Carlos Manuel de Céspedes

1878
The Peace of Zanjón grants a general amnesty to all freedom fighters. José Martí goes into exile in New York

1870-1886
Slavery is gradually replaced by cheap labour from China

1895
General Máximo Gómez and José Martí arrive in Cuba and start a second War of Independence

1898
After the *USS Maine* is blown up in Havana harbour, the US government intervenes in the dispute over sovereignty. Spain is defeated, the USA imposes a military government and secures Guantánamo as a naval base

1902
Tomás Estrada Palma becomes the first Cuban president

From 1914
The world suffers sugar shortages during the chaos of World War I; the Cuban economy prospers as a consequence

1929
The world economic crisis leads to social tensions. President Gerardo Machado uses his special troops, the *porros*, to suppress dissent. The USA intervenes

1933
Fulgencio Batista stages a coup and pulls strings behind the scenes for several different presidents. In 1940 he is elected president, but flees to Mexico four years later when he loses office

1952
Batista returns and overthrows the government of Carlos Prio Socarrás. Lawyer Fidel Castro comes to prominence as an opponent of Batista's regime

1 January 1959
Castro comes to power after a guerrilla campaign

1961
Cuban exiles land at the *Bahía de Cochinos* (Bay of Pigs) with the intention of liberating Cuba from Castro's dictatorship

1962
Cuban missile crisis: the USSR tries to station rockets with nuclear weapons on Cuba. The USA resists, and Khrushchev finally backs down

1972
Cuba becomes a member of Soviet-led Comecon

1976
New constitution and elections to the *Poder Popular* (People's Power)

1988
Celebrations are held to mark 30 years of socialism. Reforms are introduced in response to Gorbachev's policy of perestroika

1992
Intensification of economic sanctions against Cuba by the USA

1993
First secret elections to the (one-party) national assembly confirm Fidel Castro's place in office. Castro announces that he will retire in 1998

1995/6
For the first time, licences are granted to small businesses

1998
Pope Paul II visits Cuba

But Castro has always been full of surprises. In 1959, with a handful of *guerilleros,* he defeated the dictator Fulgencio Batista against all odds. Two years later the attempt by US-backed exiled Cubans to wrest power from him ended in unexpected humiliation in the Bay of Pigs. Then in the early 1990s Castro surprised everyone again by donning a businessman's suit and travelling the world in search of trade partners so that his country could evade the US boycott.

Recent policy changes have made Cuba much more accessible. Many obstacles have been cleared from the path to prosperity. Easily the largest land mass in the Caribbean (100,000 sq km or 38,600 sq mi), the island is endowed with great natural beauty. Its delightful coral beaches and tiny islands (*cayos*) are a paradise for divers and fishermen, and the fact that it has only recently opened its doors to tourism means that much of it is, as yet, unspoilt. Among its natural treasures are the Camagüey archipelago, and Varadero, east of Havana. Many of the new hotels that have been built alongside the white sandy beaches compare favourably with those that line the more fashionable resorts of the Caribbean, though hints of the mass commercialism that comes with the development of a resort are sadly creeping in.

Cuba's culture is equally rich. The island has an abundance of remarkable museums devoted to a variety of subjects, from cars to cigars, antiques to natural history, pre-Columbian archaeology to modern art. The sound of music is never far away. Wherever you go you will find the opportunity to listen and dance to salsa, son and merengue. Theatres and galleries abound and the festive calendar is packed with cultural events, from folklore festivals to film festivals.

UNESCO has also played a valuable part in preserving Cuba's culture by providing the funds for the restoration of sites of cultural interest, concentrating mainly on the historic city of Havana, which has many dilapidated and run-down quarters in desperate need of repair and restoration, the colonial gem of Trinidad (Heritage of Mankind site) in the south and the Parque

---

Events leading up to the Revolution

The history of Cuba provided the seedbed for Castro's Revolution. It had remained a colony longer than other countries in the New World. The War of Independence against Spain had taken place 100 years after similar campaigns in the northern countries of South America (Venezuela, Colombia, Ecuador). The problem in Cuba, however, was that having gained independence from Spain, the country found itself, as the young independence fighter José Martí feared, dependent on the United States; links were particularly close with the southern states such as Florida, which was not only geographically close but also shared the same Spanish roots.

In 1904 President Theodore Roosevelt reinterpreted the Monroe doctrine of 1823 to give the United States the right to intervene anywhere on the American continent. Washington was worried that the radicals would take over in Cuba. The Spanish were depicted as cruel tyrants, and the US navy helped to dislodge the weakened Spanish army. But instead of handing over control to the Cubans, the USA set up a military government to administer the country. The big brother next door was now regarded as an unloved bully. In 1912 many of the blacks who had fought for independence were killed by US marines during an uprising. The new colonial masters did nothing to even out the inequalities, and corruption, racketeering and election fraud continued unabated. It was only a matter of time before the Americans were going to be shown the door.

Nacional de Bacanao (Reserve of the Biosphere) in the east.

Surrounded by water of amazing clarity and incredible scenic beauty, it is easy to forget the problems confronting the country. But holidaymakers can take some comfort from the fact that the difficulties many Cubans face can be eased to some extent by tourism, so long as its development remains controlled and it does not end up destroying the country's identity as has so often been the case. At present this new source of income continues to yield valuable returns, and the plan is to plough back over half of the profits into the development of the tourist industry. Even at the height of revolutionary fervour, Cuba has always recognized the importance of its international friendships. As you explore the country beyond the tourist enclaves, you can't help but respect and admire its people for their friendly disposition in spite of the crises they have suffered and the poverty they must battle against.

Castro and Che Guevara watch over the Plaza de la Revolución in Havana

From architecture to tourism

*Aspects of Cuban life and culture
before and after the Revolution*

Architecture

Few cities in the American continent can compete with the architectural splendour of Havana, although neglect and the ravages of time have inflicted terrible damage on the fabric of its historic buildings. In the meantime, many of these sites have been restored, by both state and privately run enterprises. Habana Vieja or 'old Havana' is made up of neo-Baroque houses built during the sugar boom in the early 18th century. This architectural style was characterized by huge portals and marble floors and columns. Walls were covered with exquisite tiles to protect them against damp, and hard mahogany was used for ceilings and staircases. Balconies were originally also made of wood, later giving way to stone structures with ornate wrought-iron balustrades known as *rejas*. Coloured glass segments joined with lead strips became fashionable as sources of light above the doors, between walls

*Cuban girl in period garb
fashionable 500 years ago*

and in the façades behind which planted patios with airy galleries led to high-ceilinged rooms. This decorative style was replaced at the beginning of this century with extravagant *art nouveau*, *art deco* and *Bauhaus* designs.

The oldest building in Cuba is the Casa de Velázquez in Santiago de Cuba. Built in 1522, it post-dates the oldest houses in the Dominican Republic's capital of Santo Domingo by just a few years. The Spanish colonial style can be identified in the patio gallery, which is faced with floor-to-ceiling shutters.

The *bohío* – a hut of Indian origin made from clay, wooden staves, and roofed with palm leaves – has survived as the preferred structure for tourist restaurants and residential bungalows.

Beaches

Cuba's 5800 km or 3600 mile coastline boasts some 280 beaches, the best of which are found along the north coast. The coral-white beach at Varadero to the east of Havana is one of the most famous. The south coast is rockier, lined with cliffs over-

13

looking tiny bays, interrupted by the occasional expanse of beach, such as Playa Ancón near Trinidad. The offshore waters are scattered with around 1000 islands, many of them very small. The largest is the Isla de la Juventud, part of the Archipiélago de los Canarreos off the south-west coast. To the east lies the popular tourist destination, Cayo Largo. Both these islands offer excellent opportunities for diving. The Archipiélago Jardines de la Reina further east remains unspoilt. Situated off the north coast, the Archipiélago de Sabana and the Archipiélago de Camagüey have become popular with divers, especially the recently developed islands of Cayo Guillermo and Cayo Coco.

Cinema

The Cuban Film Institute, the ICAIC (Instituto Cubano del Arte e Industria Cinematográficos), enjoys a reputation which extends far beyond the Caribbean. It was led for several years by Gabriel García Márquez, the renowned Columbian writer and winner of the 1982 Nobel Prize for literature, who continues to maintain a close association with it. One of the institute's more recent productions to receive international acclaim was the award-winning *Strawberry and Chocolate.* Directed by Tomás Gutiérrez Álea and Juan Carlos Tabío, the film portrays the relationship between a homosexual and a heterosexual Cuban. It is a comic critique whose underlying message is one of tolerance. The team's follow-up film, *Guantanamera*, was screened at the 1995 International Film Festival in Venice.

Economy

When the Soviet Union collapsed, Cuba lost its main trading partner. About 70% of Cuba's exports were bought by the USSR and in return the Cubans received plentiful supplies of cheap crude oil. With Gorbachev's policy of perestroika, volumes dropped dramatically from 13 million metric tons (1989) to 3.2 million metric tons. But the cruellest blow for the Cuban economy was Boris Yeltsin's demand that oil be paid for at world market prices. The former Eastern bloc countries had been Cuba's main suppliers of cereals and meats, but imports of these fell in 1991 by 45% and 18% respectively. The markets for agricultural produce, such as tobacco, sugar, cocoa and coffee, as well as copper and nickel, have also been greatly diminished. The Cuban government is now looking to tourism to replace these important sources of income.

Fauna

More than 300 different bird species can be found on Cuba. The aura vulture quickly becomes a familiar sight. This ugly black creature about the size of a raven can be seen everywhere, circling the skies, by fields and roadsides, and is now a protected species. The national bird is the small *tocororo* whose blue, white and red plumage reflects the colours of the Cuban flag. Pheasants are hunted in the Escambray Mountains, and you can see flamingos in the lagoons of the north-east. The hot lowlands in the east are home to tiny hummingbirds, which can often be spotted hovering beside colourful flower blossoms. On the pastures of central Cuba, you will find the *garza blanca*, a small white heron which perches on grazing cattle and feeds off the parasites which live on them.

The most elusive creatures on the island are the native fireflies known as *cocuyos*. If you are lucky, you might catch a glimpse of them at night. The forests of the Sierra Maestra are the habitat of a large rodent known as the *jutía conga*. Crocodiles are farmed in the south in the marshlands of the Ciénaga de Zapata. At one time they were hunted in the wild for meat and were almost wiped out.

Ecotourism on Cuba is still in its infancy. Intensive farming has left very few parts of the country unspoilt. Among the few remaining areas of uncultivated land are La Güira National Park near Soroa and the Ciénaga de Zapata National Park, which has been a protected area for about 30 years. The manatee, an unusual sea mammal, lives in its lagoons. The Ciénaga de Zapata is also the ideal habitat for cayman monkeys and numerous species of aquatic bird. Birdwatching tours are becoming very popular in this vast wild area of mangrove forest. One of the most unusual fish to inhabit the Guamá Lagoon, also known as Treasure Lake, is the *manjuarí*. Its head resembles that of a crocodile, and it can easily be mistaken for the reptile. Over 900 different species of fish thrive in the waters off Cuba's coast.

Flora

The *palma real*, or royal palm, is typical of Cuba. It can grow to a height of 40 m (appr. 130 ft) and is easily recognized by its light, rather bulbous trunk and the bushy vertical fronds at the top. It is not to be confused with the coconut palm and produces fruit growing in thick bunches and yielding a useful oil.

Many beaches are lined by the hardy beach vine which has parchment-like, heart-shaped leaves. Before the arrival of the Spanish settlers, the native Indians held their tribal meetings beneath the foliage of the thick-trunked *ceiba* tree. This revered tree still surrounds many urban plazas. The *jagüey* fig tree comes in bizarre shapes and sizes, with aerial roots which often strangle the host tree. Pines grow at higher altitudes, and the eucalyptus tree has been planted in many regions to protect the soil from erosion. Southern European plants such as bougainvillea and oleander adorn many gardens alongside the native hibiscus. Cuba boasts some 8000 native plants, with orchids ranking among the most beautiful. The national flower is the white, strongly-scented *mariposa* or butterfly jasmine.

Food supplies

The task of keeping the population supplied with food is, generally speaking, run from the centre by a bureaucracy. Whatever cooperatives and small enterprises produce for the Cuban people is distributed by coupons or *libreta* – the goods in question range from milk for children through to soap and shoes. Usually the *libreta* are of little value, as many items are strictly rationed or simply not available anyway. But the black market and, more recently, the opening up of the economy to small businesses have enabled Cubans to bypass the system and to keep their cupboards and shelves well stocked. With a quasi-free market system, the economy is receiving a welcome boost, and the state is also benefiting as every trader with a licence is obliged to hand over 10% of the profits as what is, in effect, income tax.

Government

Cuba is a socialist republic with a one-party system. The only party allowed to exist here is the Communist Party of Cuba (PCC). The National Assembly, made up of 589 representatives elected by the people, serves as the nation's parliament. Cuba's commander-in-chief and head of state is Fidel Castro. In 1992 the People's Congress reformed 76 aspects of the constitution. Since then, direct elections have taken place, and state-owned properties have been allowed to pass into private ownership. The head of state's earlier right to call, at any time, a state of emergency in the event of external threats or internal disorder was abolished. Religious freedom was also guaranteed.

Landscape

Apart from the eastern Sierra Maestra, whose highest point is the Pico Turquino (2005 m/6615 ft), and the lower mountain region of Guamuhaya and the Cordillera Guaniguanico in the west, Cuba is either flat or gently undulating with little woodland to speak of. Cuban poet Nicolás Guillén compared its shape to a crocodile.

At the heart of the island, extensive fields of sugar cane and pastureland stretch to the horizon. Black and white cattle graze peacefully in the meadows and the view is only broken by small villages and military training camps. Royal palm trees, a characteristic feature of the Cuban skyline, dot the countryside. Little water flows along the many rivers, which are never far from the sea. They often disappear underground, cutting channels through the chalky rock, and rising to the surface again at another point. When watercourses have been dammed, as with the Hanabanilla reservoir, the river landscape becomes a scene of melancholy beauty. The tropical Ciénaga de Zapata is always wet.

The densest vegetation is to be found in the east in the Sierra Maestra, where the *guerilleros* first hid following their arrival from Mexico. The hot climate and the steep hillsides are ideal for the cultivation of coffee and cocoa. Conifers also thrive at the higher altitudes.

The *mogotes* in the west have a special charm. These flat- or round-topped limestone mounds which rise up out of the plain are dotted with caverns and subterranean rivers and date back to the Jurassic period. It is in this region that the best tobacco in the world is produced.

Literature

Cuba is often associated with the literary giants Graham Greene and Ernest Hemingway. Both chose Cuba as the setting for a novel. But, unlike Greene, the American writer lived on Cuba for a while and it was here that he wrote his celebrated short story *The Old Man and the Sea*.

Alejo Carpentier is perhaps the best known of Cuba's own novelists. Born in Havana in 1904 he later lived in France, but then

The Hemingway Museum on the outskirts of Havana is full of 'Don Ernesto' memorabilia

moved to Caracas in 1945. After the Revolution he returned to Cuba to become director of the state publishing house. In 1966 he was appointed Cuban cultural attaché in Paris, where he died in 1980. His first novel *Ecué-Yamba-O* is about rival magicians of the Santoría cult. Nicolás Guillén (1902-89) probably ranks as the most influential Cuban literary figure, but contemporary writers such as Mañuel Pereira and Norberto Fuentes are gaining ground. Thanks to the intervention of Castro's friend García Márquez, Fuentes, author of *Hemingway in Cuba,* was actually given permission to travel abroad. He once spent 20 days in prison for 'inappropriate behaviour'. Another writer, Jesús Díaz, was forced into exile after making some critical remarks. He now lives in Berlin.

Music

Cuban music has its roots in Afro-Spanish rhythms. It has been popular in Europe since the 1800s and later gained a following in the USA. Havana occupied a key position as a bridgehead between Europe and the New World, and is now regarded as the capital of Latin American music. Even the tango, which came to prominence in Argentina, originated in Cuba.

Most of the best-known Latin American dances, such as the mambo, the cha-cha-cha and the salsa, started life on Cuba. The musical talent of the Cubans was recognized by their colonial masters, who were always happy to let a few slaves play background music at social events. They would have used either their own instruments or ones imported from Europe. The dances that the black musicians devised were often adaptations of European movements. The conga, for example, initially viewed by the white colonialists as a vulgar slave dance, eventually became socially acceptable. Conversely, the *zapateado,* a Spanish-style minuet, was reinterpreted as an African dance.

The great wave of interest in Latin American dancing which spread from Cuba to the USA and on to Europe was preceded by the *danzón*, a blend of Afro-French and Spanish movements that emerged around the turn of the century. This was followed by the rumba, a dance which is synonymous throughout Latin America with 'letting go'. However, the rumba that was taught in European dance schools from the 1930s to the 1950s had little in common with the original dance.

Son and salsa are still very much alive in Cuba and it is not difficult to find venues where they can be heard (e.g. the Palacio de la Salsa in the Habana Riviera hotel). Authentic Cuban salsa is more reliant on the acoustic guitar and percussion than in other parts of Latin America where the sound is 'brassier'. One Cuban song, *Guantanamera*, written in 1929 by Joseita Fernandez with lyrics by José Martí, was first performed outside Cuba by Pete Seeger, at a concert in New York in 1963 as a gesture of solidarity with the Cuban people. Its delightful melody is now familiar across the world and is even chanted on our football terraces.

Since the Revolution, protest songs and thoughtful but down-to-earth ballads have become very popular, in much the same way that songs by the master of the 'Nueva Trova Cubana', Carlos Puebla, were when he performed in the cafés of Havana during the Batista regime. The latest music trends are a mixture of Cuban styles with strong rock elements. The group Irakere are the most popular exponents of this new Cuban music.

Population

Cuba's population is currently estimated at 10.3 million. Approximately 70% of Cubans are white (mostly of Spanish origin), 12% black (descendants of African slaves), 17% are *mestizos* or mulattos and 0.1% are of Chinese origin.

The Revolution instilled an awareness of equal rights in all classes of the population. This awareness manifests itself in the calm, respectful way the people treat each other, and in the fact that machismo is much less pronounced here than in the rest of Latin America.

Revolution

Fidel Castro was born in Mayari (Oriente Province) on 13 August 1927. He first came to prominence after Batista illegally assumed power in 1952. Although he had only just graduated from law school, Castro challenged Batista's right to rule in the courts. The dictator employed many brutal tactics to suppress opposition and had many influential friends in the United States. When Castro's challenge was ignored by the unpopular government, he started to plan the despot's downfall. He had no difficulty gathering together a number of intellectuals and, on 26 July 1953, Castro led 150 rebels in an armed attack against the Moncada barracks, an important military base in Santiago de Cuba; it was a disaster. When the population learned that the captured rebels were being murdered and tortured, the *July 26th Movement* was founded. Castro made a passionate speech in his own defence, railing against the injustices of the Batista government, but he was sentenced to 15 years in jail. Following a public outcry, he was released and fled to Mexico, where he met the Argentinian doctor, Ernesto Guevara, otherwise known as Che. They shared the same political ideals and soon set about planning the overthrow of the Cuban government. On 2 December 1956, Castro, Guevara and 80 other revolutionaries landed on Cuba. Again, disaster struck. The insurrectionists were betrayed and most of them died, but Castro and Che Guevara were among the survivors. After withdrawing into the Sierra Maestra, the leaders continued to plot against the government in Havana. They used the pirate station *Radio Rebelde* to denounce Batista, and quickly built up a powerful guerrilla force. Batista declared that Castro was dead, but an interview in the *New York Times* proved that he was very much alive, and that his movement was growing in strength. Batista soon recognized that he could no longer rely on his army. He resorted to torture and oppression, but that merely served to undermine his authority even more. Castro's guerrillas mounted ever fiercer attacks and eventually seized the important central town of Santa Clara. On 1 January 1959, Batista fled Havana with millions of dollars, appropriated through corruption, stuffed into suitcases. On 8 January Fidel Castro entered Havana.

Cuba's road to Communism

The main aims of the Revolution, in the eyes of Castro and his comrades, were social reform and national independence. That the two were not always compatible was something that the new leaders soon had to come to terms with. The social reforms after the Revolution started with the confiscation of the assets of foreign companies. Owners were promised compensation, but the government was not consistent. Canadian companies, for example, were not penalized, but when the USA applied sanctions in the form of the OAS's trade embargo, the Cuban authorities were all the harsher towards American firms. The power struggle came to a head in 1962 with the Cuban missile crisis, when Cuba gave the Soviet Union permission to station rockets in the country. What precisely happened to bring the crisis to a peaceful conclusion is not clear, but the rockets were dismantled. Nevertheless, Cuba was now a plaything for the two superpowers. In the end, of course, Castro became dependent on the Russians. Che Guevara left Cuba in 1965, ostensibly so that he could continue the revolutionary struggle in South America, and he was later killed. So Castro was left on his own to resolve the mounting problems. He decided to intensify the revolutionary process with an almost puritanical zeal, banning private enterprise and the entertainment business, introducing the collective harvest and punishment for the work-shy. Now, over 30 years later, Castro's strict interpretation of communist ideology is viewed as a tribute to his friend and adviser, Che Guevara.

Social issues

The road to Cuban socialism began with agrarian and social reform. Landowners with more than 400 hectares (980 acres), and those who owned more than one house, had their excess land and property confiscated. This was then redistributed to the needy. The lowest strata of the population benefited from a massive literacy programme. Schooling, higher education and medical provision were (and still are) free, and workers initially enjoyed job security. Today, however, the unemployed are entitled to only 30% of their previous wage, and children at nurseries and boarding schools have to pay for their meals. Thanks to the comprehensive education system, 94% of all Cubans can read and write. Medical care is quite good : there is one doctor for every 1000 Cubans, and infant mortality rates are on a par with many western European countries. However, more and more doctors and other highly qualified workers have had to abandon their professions because of the low pay, and are now forced to work in the tourist industry.

Sugar

Sugar cane was first introduced to Cuba by Christopher Columbus and has been cultivated on a large scale since the late 18th century. Huge expanses of land were cleared so that landowners could benefit from the high worldwide demand. By 1791, Cuba was the world's largest producer of sugar and the USA's main supplier. After the Revolution, Cuba became the Soviet Union's main source of sugar. Now the commodity is used in barter agreements with Russia, China,

Back-breaking work on the sugar plantation

20

Canada, and the country's new trading partners in Europe. The *zafra* harvest takes place in the dry season (November to May), and most of the work is done by hand. The juice or *guarapo* extracted from the crushed stems is boiled down until sugar crystals form. Molasses, one of the by-products of the refining process, is used to make rum. After fermentation and distillation, the rum is left to mature in wooden barrels made from Canadian oak. White rum needs about three years to reach maturity, brown rum requires 15.

Tobacco

This native plant was used by the Indians for ritual ceremonies. Christopher Columbus appreciated its attractions and brought some samples back to Europe. During the 16th century, smoking became a social pastime for the wealthy. Thanks to the favourable soil conditions, the western province of Pinar del Río is generally reckoned to produce the best tobacco in the world. The leaves are left to grow for about three months and then they are harvested, sorted and left to dry in storerooms or on racks. If they are moistened with water regularly, an even fermentation process is guaranteed. There are no fewer than 15 different qualities of tobacco. *Hojas negras*, the dark leaves, are said to be the best. Cigars are rolled by hand. If you pay a visit to one of the many cigar factories in Cuba, you can watch the skilled *tabaqueros* at work. There are about 80 different stages involved in the making of a good cigar, which is why a box of the best cigars can cost as much as $200.

Tourism

Cuba was slow to appreciate the value of tourism as a source of hard currency. But 'joint ventures' are now seen as the key to the nation's survival. German, Spanish, Dutch, Italian and French companies have foreseen Cuba's unique attractions and have invested millions of dollars in hotels and infrastructure. In 1997 tourist numbers rose to approximately 1,430,000 (an increase of 530,000 on the previous year). Compared to other Caribbean islands, Cuba currently boasts the highest growth rate. Presently, Cuba offers some 28,000 tourist beds, which exceeds the number previously planned for. Thus, Cuba's ambitious goal of being able to accommodate 2 million visitors each year by the year 2000 is beginning to look realistic. Protests against this development have already started: abroad, from quarters where mass tourism is frowned upon, and at home, where there are fears about social cohesion and a 'weakening of ideology through foreign influences' (Defence minister Raúl Castro, April 1996).

US Trade Embargo

In the early 1960s, soon after the first US company was nationalized in the post-Revolution period, the American government imposed a trade embargo. In 1992 US President George Bush widened the embargo. If a vessel had carried goods to or from Cuba, then it could only enter an American harbour if it had received express permission from the American Finance Ministry. It was hoped that Bill Clinton might relax this policy, but as yet there have been few changes.

Seafood and Cuba Libre

Iced rum cocktails and sexy Salsa rhythms will soon help you forget the food shortages

One lime, six to eight large fresh mint leaves crushed with sugar, 2 cl of the best rum, soda water, ice, and a sprig of mint – mix it all together and you have Cuba's delicious national drink, Hemingway's beloved *mojito*. Or how about a pale green daiquiri made from sugar cane syrup, rum, lemon juice, and crushed ice? Then, of course, there's the *Cuba libre*, rum and coke on ice, first mixed in celebration of Cuban independence at the turn of the century. These are the three Cuban classics, but there are dozens of other cocktails you can choose from, all of them rum-based. Ask for a Mary Pickford, a Havana Special, or a *canchanchara*. As you sit sipping your refreshing cocktail in a humid Havana bar you can easily imagine the atmosphere of these notorious mafia haunts in the days when Al Capone and Meyer Lansky were regular visitors, not to mention the heavy-drinking Ernest Hemingway.

Hemingway's favourite Havana haunt serves more than just 'mojito'

Havana's cocktail bars still thrive on the memories of those legendary Prohibition years, when the production and sale of alcohol was forbidden in the USA (1920-33). At that time, alcohol consumption was legal in Cuba, and so Havana became a popular meeting place for serious drinkers and with them all the underworld criminals and gangsters who profited from the alcohol ban. These haunts are now very popular with tourists, who bring desperately-needed hard currency. Hemingway's favourite bars, such as La Bodeguita del Medio and the El Floridita, are now obligatory stopping places for any visitor to Havana. But even the hotels know how to cultivate this side of Cuba's history, and you will see bartenders across the country proudly adopt that typical pose as they mix their own special concoction for you.

An essential ingredient in any Havana cocktail is genuine Cuban rum, be it white or *añejo* (brown). Matured for three, five, seven or 15 years in oak casks, it ranges in colour from golden yellow to caramel brown depending on its age. Bacardi, the world's most famous rum, originates in Cuba. Its distillers put the emphasis on quality, starting at the very root of the process. Like the tobacco plants cultivated for Havana cigars, the Bacardi sugar cane was only grown on the best quality soil. According to legend, American businessmen used to meet at the Havana Club, where the Bacardi rum-distilling dynasty would lavish free rum on their guests. After the Revolution, the Bacardis fled to Puerto Rico, but Cuba still cherishes the legacy of this, perhaps the most famous, dynasty that went into exile in the late 1950s. What many people do not realize is that the Bacardi family were, in fact, well disposed towards social reform and had even lent Castro money for the Revolution – after which he, of course, confiscated their land. The legendary club where many a big business deal was clinched is now immortalized in the popular 'Habana Club' rum.

Beer drinkers will not be disappointed by the fine Cuban brews. There are several different varieties, of which Hatuey and Mayabe are the best known.

Cuban coffee or *café cubano* is traditionally taken strong, black and very sweet, and is served in tiny cups, much like espresso. *Café con leche* (coffee with milk), usually taken for breakfast, is the same strong coffee in a large cup topped with hot milk.

Guarapo is the name of the cloudy, sweet juice of the sugar cane. It is a very popular drink served freshly squeezed from the cane stalks with plenty of ice and lime to counter the sweetness. In bars, markets and by the beach you will come across traders (who have been granted licences from the state) with their wonderful juice-extracting contraptions. Despite its sweetness, *guarapo* is very refreshing, and is also rich in protein.

The choice of tropical fruit juices and fresh fruit has improved considerably in recent times. As well as lemons, oranges and grapefruit, *piñas* (pineapple), mangoes, pawpaw and guava are usually available.

While you will not be disappointed on the drinks front, Cuban food is a different matter. Food supplies are generally very short, though this of course is not the case in large hotels. You may find that the restaurants – *ranchos* or *rancheros* – mentioned in this guide are indeed open, but that only a small selection of foods may be on offer, and even then you cannot always expect to be able to order what is shown on the menu. It all depends what ingredients the kitchen has access to that day. Many of the smaller tourist restaurants, which have opened up recently between Viñales and Santiago de Cuba, suffer badly from inadequate food supplies and energy shortages – several have even been forced to close.

Nevertheless, some restaurants seem to survive without any food supply problems, and manage to make do well enough with whatever is to hand. Cubans love to eat meat, and there never seems to be a shortage of chicken, which is usually fried in oil and served with a crispy skin. Europeans often prefer roast (*asado*). Pork is also very popular. Meat dishes are

A feast for the eyes: lobsters are a local treat but overfished due to tourist demand

usually served with rice and black beans, *arroz moro* – supplies of these two ingredients never seem to run out. Sweet potatoes (*malanga* or *boniato*), yams (*ñame*) or manioc (*yuca*) are often served as a vegetable. All were cultivated by the native Indians as important sources of energy. Fried *plátanos,* or cooking bananas, often accompany fish and meat.

Strongly influenced by Spanish-Moorish culinary customs, traditional Cuban fare often includes soup. One original Spanish classic, which frequently appears on menus, is the simple but delicious *sopa de ajo,* or garlic soup. The Cubans also know how to make hearty warming stews out of pumpkin (*calabaza*), onions, sweetcorn and black beans (*frijoles*).

For many tourists, the highlight of the limited Cuban culinary repertoire is seafood. Lobsters (*langosta*) never seem to be in short supply, at least not in the hotels and coastal resorts. Lobster stocks are, however, depleting fast in the surrounding waters because of the amount fished to feed tourists. Fish is either boiled (*hervido*), baked (*asado*), piled on to a pizza, fried in batter, or served in a salad (*salpicón*). One Cuban speciality to look out for is *arroz con pescado al ron,* rice with fish marinated in rum with cloves, pepper, oregano or bay leaf, and garlic.

You may well be approached on the street and asked if you are looking for a *paladar* — a private restaurant which is often no more than a few tables in the courtyard of someone's home. There are an increasing number of these little restaurants in operation and, although it is sometimes a gamble, the food they serve is often of a much higher quality than you will find in the state-run restaurants. Some do not have written menus, and you should establish the price (in dollars) beforehand.

Havana cigars, Cuban rhythms

An increasing number of colourful markets, hotel shops and art galleries to tempt you into parting with your dollars

Cuba's shop windows are not as spartan as you might expect, but the goods on display are somewhat limited. Most of the larger hotels have souvenir shops in the lobby, which sell mainly cigars, Che Guevara T-shirts and other 'Che' memorabilia, books about the Revolution, assorted jewellery and newly-pressed CDs made in Canada featuring all kinds of Cuban rhythms from bolero to son.

There is no shortage of souvenir outlets in Cuba as a whole, especially in Havana. A good starting point for shopping in the capital is the Plaza de Armas in Habana Vieja, near the port. A second-hand book market is held here at weekends. Most of the books are, of course, in Spanish, but some collectors' items can be found, and it makes for interesting browsing. Leading off the square is the bustling Calle del Obispo. If you stroll down this street you will come to the pottery studio of a

You can buy Cuban and Afro-Cuban works of art at the ACAA in Havana

respected local artist, which is worth a visit even if it's just to admire his work. Further up, on the left-hand side (no. 411), you'll find the sales gallery of the Asociación Cubana de Artesanos Artistas (ACAA), the Federation of Cuban Artisans. The exhibits, sold only for dollars, show Cuban creativity at its best. You can find some unusual and imaginative pieces made from local materials, such as sisal, cedar and mahogany, shells, palm leaves and papier mâché. Take a look at the giant chicken, for example, an ironic symbol of Latin American masculine pride magnificently painted in bright traditional colours. Admire the award-winning sculpture, a finely crafted tall figure that incorporates all 20 Afro-Cuban deities (*orishas*).

Should you decide to invest in some Cuban art, you can arrange for bulky items to be packed in a crate and shipped direct to your home, though there is no guarantee how long this will take. Authentic works of art can cost in excess of $100, and carriage is not cheap, but that should not deter the serious buyer.

A 'tabaquero' at work in one of the country's many cigar factories, spurred along by the aroma of a fat Havana

Cheaper and much easier to transport is the finely crafted silver and shell jewellery produced by the ACAA artists. Among the other crafts on display in the gallery are works by wood and textile designers, sisal tapestries in well-coordinated colours and weaving styles, sculptures of Afro-Cuban mythological figures, and rather striking papier mâché demon masks.

An increasing number of market stalls now liven up the urban squares across the country. Such markets are mainly aimed at tourists, but they are a good source of gifts and souvenirs. The main market in Havana is set up on the cathedral square, Plaza de la Catedral. The atmosphere here is lively and colourful, and the stall holders will try to coax you into buying a whole range of useful and useless things. Jewellery made from shells and silver wire, or wood and coral, reproductions of Spanish sailing ships, percussion instruments, crocheted tops and dresses, painted plates, woven straw bags and shoes, woodcarvings, painted dolls, etc. Amateur painters seeking to outdo each other with romantic sunsets, landscapes, and naive paintings display their works on the far side of the square.

If you join one of the organized excursions, you will be taken to the state-run 'Caracol' souvenir shops identified by the snail shell symbol. Mainly located in Havana and Varadero, these and the Artex shops overflow with potential gifts and mementoes. You can pick up some unusual things such as garden or children's furniture woven from dried sisal leaves, creative jewellery, Creole dolls and naive art.

Motorway service stations are a good place to buy CDs. They stock a relatively wide range of albums at a reasonable price (around $17). Look out for a series of compilations entitled *Antología de la música Cubana*. Produced in Canada and distributed under the Artex label, the collection is available on CD and cassette. There are currently four in the series. Each one comes with its own sleeve notes (in Spanish) written by a music specialist from the Museo Nacional de la Música in Havana, which provide authoritative background information.

The best place to buy top quality Havana cigars is from one of the many cigar factories (*fábricas de tabaco*), where you can watch the *tabaqueros* at work. They sit at what look like wooden school benches and roll out the ripe leaves on boards of mango wood. Different types of leaves are arranged in different positions inside the cigar. Once they have been rolled and trimmed, the cigars are then graded by the placing of an *anillo* or paper ring around the perimeter. They are then carefully boxed in cedarwood before undergoing a final quality-control inspection. If you don't make it to one of the cigar factories, most hotels have their own resident cigar makers. Guests are free to watch the *tabaqueros* at work, but no commentary is given. Visiting a factory is a much livelier way of learning about the rituals behind the making of a cigar.

The first tobacco smokers were the Indios Hispaniolas. Among the most famous 20th century aficionados of the Havana were Winston Churchill, Che Guevara – who despite his asthma loved the strong *puros* type – and, of course, Fidel Castro himself. Havanas continue to be regarded by connoisseurs as the best cigars in the world. This is largely down to the composition of the soil. The Pinar del Río region, for example, is reckoned to be perfect for growing tobacco leaves. Other factors such as care of the plant, duration and nature of storage, right up to fermentation, also play an important role. Every planter has his own recipe that has been handed down through generations.

Cuba is also the cheapest place in the world to buy Havanas, which cost from $3 per cigar. The best brand names are Montecristo and Upmann.

If you want to bring the taste of Cuba back home with you, you can't do better than a bottle of rum (Havana Club), and a packet of Cuban coffee. Both can be found in most souvenir shops and at the airport.

Consumer goods of western origin, e.g. camera batteries, films and portable radios, are sold in 'Tiendas'. The only currency accepted in these shops is the American dollar.

Opening times: Shops, *Mon-Sat 12.30-19.30*; Tourist shops, *daily 10.00-21.00*; Banks and bureaux de change, *Mon-Fri 08.30-12.00 and 13.30-15.00*; Post offices (*Correos*), *Mon-Fri 08.00-18.00*; Shops in the Servi petrol stations stay open 24 hours a day.

Music and masquerades

*The raucous carnivals and festivals make a welcome change
from the more sombre revolutionary celebrations*

In Santiago de Cuba every Saturday is Rumba Saturday or ★ *Sábado de Rumba*. The street is closed to traffic and a band plays while dancers of all ages perform with enviable style and natural rhythm. Large crowds fill the rows of seats lined up behind the stage and the family atmosphere slowly builds up to fever pitch. A communal rumba at the state's expense. No one wanders round cap in hand asking for donations. The musicians are paid for by the town council and the whole event is arranged by the local cultural committee. Similar street festivals take place in almost every town in Cuba.

Nothing ever seems to destroy the Cubans' innate *joie de vivre*. Even the frequent days of remembrance for the victims of the revolutionary struggle inevitably turn into lively occasions. Many of these secular festivals have replaced religious events. The public holiday calendar is now dominated by the remembrance of numerous significant revolutionary events. Prior to the Revolution, Cuba was essentially a Catholic country, but the church and the state are now completely separate. Holy Week or *Semana Santa*, for example, does not appear in the official events calendar. That is not to say, however, that religion has been abandoned. An Afro-Cuban form of Catholicism is still practised here, but commemorative days are generally celebrated in private.

The major attractions for visitors are the Havana carnival which takes place in July, and the even more spectacular Santiago de Cuba carnival at the end of July/beginning of August. On this occasion, exuberant masked dancers twist and turn their way through the narrow alleys as the constant sound of beating drums rings through the air and crowds of people gather together to watch and join in the fun.

Cuba enjoys its carnivals much more than many of its Caribbean neighbours and more emphasis is placed on the artistic element of the festivities. Many of these fest-

The stresses and strains of life are alleviated on the dance floor: rhythm is in the Cuban blood

MARCO POLO SELECTION: EVENTS

1 Carnival in Santiago de Cuba
Dancers, masked parades, processions and rumba – end of July/beginning of August (page 33)

2 Music festival in Varadero
Salsa, son, bolero, and new Latin American rock – every other year in November (page 33)

3 Film festival in Havana
Latin Americas top cultural event, screening films from Brazil to Uruguay (page 33)

4 Sábado de Rumba
Festival for everyone in Santiago de Cuba with local bands and dancing in the streets (page 31)

ivals have gained international renown. The *Festival Internacional del Nuevo Cine Latinoamericano* (International Festival of New Latin American Films), which is held in Havana every December, is particularly well-respected and nearly every country in Latin America takes part. Other important festivals include the *Concurso Festival Internacional de Guitarra* (International Guitar Competition) which takes place every other year in Havana, the *Festival Internacional de Música Popular Benny More* (International Benny More Folk Music Festival) in Cienfuegos, the annual Cuban literature prize-giving ceremony, and the *Festival Internacional de Jazz Plaza* (International Jazz Festival), and have, culturally speaking, put Cuba very firmly on the Caribbean map. For the exact dates of these events, contact the *Centro Cultural Cubanacán, Calle 21, e/Ave. Playa, Varadero; Tel: 05/ 632 98.*

HOLIDAYS

The official non-working days are marked in the following list with an asterisk (*).

1 January* *Día de la Liberación* (Liberation Day)

28 January *Nacimiento de José Martí* (Birthday of the national hero)

14 February *Día de los Enamorados* (Lovers' Day)

24 February *Aniversario del comienzo de la segunda etapa de la Guerra de Independencia en 1895* (Commemoration of the beginning of the second phase of the war of independence in 1895)

8 March *Día de la mujer* (International Women's Day)

13 March *Aniversario del ataque al palacio Presidencial de La Habana* (Commemoration of the attack on the presidential palace in Havana)

19 April *Victory in the Bay of Pigs*, 1961

1 May* *Labour Day* (Speech by Fidel Castro)

Second Sunday in May, *Día de la madre* (Mother's Day)

Third Sunday in June *Día del padre* (Father's Day)

25–27 July* *Día de la Rebeldía Nacional* (Day of the attack on Moncada barracks)

30 July* Day of the martyrs of the Revolution

8 September *Day of the patron saint of Cuba, the Virgen de la Claridad*

8 October *Death of Che Guevara*

10 October *Aniversario de las Guerras de Independencia* (Wars of Independence Day)

28 October *Anniversary of the death of Camilo Cienfuegos*

First Sunday in November, *Domingo Rojo* (Red Sunday, a voluntary workday in commemoration of the October Revolution)

27 November *Commemoration of the murder of eight medical students by the Spanish colonial government in 1871*

7 December *Death of Antonio Maceo*, who fell during the War of Independence in 1896

EVENTS

January/February

Second week in January until February: *Tourists' Carnival* in Varadero

April

Festival del Caribe del Pregón in Santiago de Cuba

June

Cultura Caribena, Afro-Cuban festival in Santiago de Cuba, usually held at the beginning of June.

Folk music in the Casa de Trova in Ciego de Ávila

For further information: *Calle 13, no. 154, Vista Alegre, Santiago de Cuba; Tel: 0226/422 85 and 423 87*

Jornada Cucalambeana, folklore festival with traditional folk dancing in Las Tunas

July

Third Sunday in July: *Día de los Niños*, children's day with carnival

18 July until beginning of August: *Carnival in Havana*

25 July: start of 10-day ★ *carnival* in Santiago de Cuba

August

Festival de Teatro de la Habana, usually end of August until beginning of September. For further information: *Calle 4 between Calle 11 and Calle 13, Vedado, Ciudad de la Habana; Tel: 07/30 43 51, 30 33 21-29*

October

Fiesta de la Cultura Iberoamericana, lectures, videos, exhibitions in Holguín

November

Every second year: ★ *International Music Festival* in Varadero

Festival Internacional de Ballet, International Ballet Festival. For further information: *road between Calle D and Calle E, Vedado, Ciudad de la Havana; Tel: 07/30 99 02*

December

★ *Festival Internacional del Nuevo Cine Latinoamericano,* International Festival of New Latin American Films in Havana

Festival Internacional de Coros, International Choir Festival in Santiago de Cuba

End December: *Parrandas* (processions) in Remedios

The heart of culture and commerce

Faded colonial splendour, lush tobacco fields,
fine coral beaches and tropical islands

At first glance Havana, once the proud but notorious queen of the Caribbean, appears worn down and weakened by the country's long battle for survival. The old town, still in a sorry state compared to its former grandeur, is increasingly being restored and reflects Cuba's difficulties in trying to come to terms with a rapidly changing world. Though crumbling at the edges, Havana still has an air of splendour about it, and

A vintage American car, a familiar but increasingly rare sight in Havana's old town

few can deny that for all its problems it is a captivating place. Be prepared to be hassled by locals trying to sell you their services, but it's a nuisance worth enduring: as you explore the backstreets and piece together the city's history you will discover many hidden treasures. Havana's plight is far from hopeless and you can really sense an appetite for change. Recent initiatives have brought fresh hope to the irrepressible Cuban people, who have restored many of the fine old inner-city buildings, alleyways and squares where little markets now flourish.

Hotel and Restaurant Prices

Hotels
Category 1: over $120
Category 2: over $60
Category 3: less than $60
Prices per person per night in double room without breakfast

Restaurants
Category 1: over $15
Category 2: over $10
Category 3: less than $10
Price per head for a meal, ie starter, main course, dessert, but no drink

Finding addresses

Ave.	Avenida (Avenue)	**e/** stands for 'entre' which means
esq.	on the corner of	between (two streets)

These new commercial developments are much further advanced in Varadero, the main resort, which is a two-hour drive east of Havana. The magnificent stretch of beach has been transformed by foreign investors from a quiet resort used by local people into an international resort visited by tourists from all over Europe, Canada and Latin America. This town, whose shimmering horizon of turquoise sea and broad coral beach have long attracted writers and artists, seems to be changing by the day. New hotels, a lick of paint on old walls, and a new entrepreneurial spirit, national and international, behind shop counters have turned Varadero into a place with a lively, almost western feel.

Ciénaga de Zapata on the opposite coast is ecologically Cuba's most precious region. Just offshore lies Cayo Largo, a paradise island dedicated to 'new tourism'. Both can be visited on organized excursions from Havana and Varadero.

The western province of Pinar del Río is easily accessible by car. This trip will take you well away from urban life and deep into tobacco country. The town of Pinar lies in an area of unique charm. This is where you will find the *mogotes:* flat-topped mountains covered in luxuriant foliage. These huge mounds of hard stone were left standing as the surrounding softer soil eroded away over millions of years. Some have a network of caves which can be explored by boat. In others, dancers perform beneath the impressive stalactites.

The second-largest island in the Cuban archipelago, the Isla de la Juventud, can be reached by plane from Havana. It acquired its name, the 'Isle of Youth', in 1978 in acknowledgement of its role as an educational centre, which consists of a teacher training college and numerous boarding schools. The island's main attraction for tourists is diving. The reefs which surround what is often referred to as 'Treasure Island' are a dream come true for diving enthusiasts. Many a pirate ship tried to plunder vessels leaving the wealthy port of Havana, only to founder on the rocks. Divers still scour the wrecks for the remnants of their precious cargo.

HAVANA

(102/C 2) 'If you did not experience the days before the Revolution, then you cannot know the joys of life.' These words were not spoken by a Cuban landowner, but by statesman Talleyrand after the French Revolution. In Havana, the beautifully restored historic buildings in the city centre serve as reminders of the prerevolutionary joys of life as experienced by the sugar cane and tobacco plantation aristocracy. For some time now the city has been gripped by a new revolution, which has been described as the change from 'red' socialism to 'green' socialism. Everywhere buildings are being restored, new hotels and restaurants are emerging, and the streets are alive with souvenir sellers.

There are few other towns in Latin America that have such a history of contrasting fortunes. La Habana, as the Cubans call it, is the island's capital and, with a population of three million, its largest city. It was founded in 1519 by Diego Velázquez, a few years after Santo Domingo in what is now the Dominican Republic. From the early days it was the trading centre for the Spanish 'New World' and later of the colonies that Spain retained in the face of rivalry from other European powers. No city or country remained under Spanish rule for as long as Havana and Cuba did. It is hard to believe, but less than a hundred years ago the palaces here were still occupied by dukes and counts, just as they had been for centuries. They had amassed untold wealth on the back of cheap labour. Grand façades and

portals, elegant inner courtyards and a luxurious lifestyle characterized by Rococo, Louis XVI and Empire furniture (on display in the museums) are a testament to the colonial attitudes that survived on Cuba until the early 20th century.

By the end of the 18th century, the relaxed urban way of life of Havana's old town had gradually spread across the bay of the peninsula. Both sides of the Bahía de la Habana were well protected against pirates by the Castillo del Morro and the Castillo de la Punta and further inland by the Fortaleza de la Cabaña and the Castillo de la Real Fuerza.

In the early 19th century, Havana started to grow beyond its old city walls and out towards the west, where the Plaza de la Revolución, La Rampa, Havana's main shopping street, and the rest of the present-day city centre lie. The Malecón, originally part of the old town fortifications, runs along the coast for several kilometres as far as the tourist districts of Vedado and Miramar. Beyond them it becomes the 5a Avenida, lined by 1940s villas that now house foreign embassies. The modern Marina Hemingway lies on the furthest edge of the city.

For centuries, the western shore of the Bahía de la Habana was excluded from new development, but a tunnel now crosses the bay at its narrowest point, emerging close to the enlarged sports ground 'Complejo Panamericano' which was used for the 1991 Pan-American games. To the north-east, the pretty fishing village of Cojímar nestles beside a small bay. This was one of Hemingway's favourite spots

The Castillo del Morro was built to protect Havana from pirates

and he often used it as a base for his many fishing trips. *La Terraza* restaurant was his favourite haunt. After his *finca* in San Francisco de Paula, 10 km (6 mi) south of Havana, Cojímar is the most popular destination for short excursions from Havana.

For most tourists, the old town is Havana's main attraction. Narrow streets overlooked by tall Baroque and classical-style buildings dominate the Ciudad Vieja. Visitors can stroll along old, cobbled streets passing huge double doors through which they can glimpse magnificent entrance halls, and into colonnaded *patios*, look across courtyards where the nobility parked their carriages, walk upon marble floors, run their hand across gently curving banisters of elegant mahogany and enter rooms as large and as high as church naves, where the walls are hung with gilded mirrors and the ceilings drip with heavy crystal-glass chandeliers. The museums and historic buildings are manned by staff dressed in grey uniforms or sober, creased suits. Policemen stand nonchalantly on the street corners. Old men and women sit on doorsteps savouring their cigars. Cuban girls in short skirts stroll up and down the pavements like high-spirited schoolchildren, while the men look on casually and chat away amongst themselves, quite unimpressed. Nowhere else can you observe the carefree nature of the Cuban as readily as in Havana's old town.

The best starting point for a tour of the old quarter is the Plaza de Armas. The former main shopping street, Calle del Obispo leads off it, and just around the corner is the narrow Plaza de la Catedral, which resembles the backdrop for a medieval play. Something of a Mediterranean atmosphere pervades the area around the Parque Central, the Baroque Teatro García Lorca and the Hotel Inglaterra fronted by a fine array of royal palms. This is heightened by the breaths of salty air you catch as you wander down the Paseo del Prado, paved with mosaics, to the harbour front. In the evenings, Cuban menfolk, courting couples, mothers with children and teenagers eating ice cream and wheeling bicycles, all congregate around the wall beside the promenade. Street lamps bathe the Malecón in soft light, while the columned houses opposite and the old town beyond are barely lit.

In 1982, UNESCO declared Havana's old town a World Heritage Site. For over 10 years now this architectural legacy has been undergoing restoration. Despite the fact that the former splendour reawakens unhappy memories of colonialism, corruption and despotic rule, the rebuilding work is universally popular. Gone are the days of pre-revolutionary chaos, of ricocheting bullets and of torture in the prisons of the Cuban dictator Batista – days brought to life so vividly in the Hollywood film *Havana*, starring Robert Redford.

SIGHTS

Calle del Obispo (U/F3)

❁ Once Havana's main shopping area, the Calle del Obispo has been undergoing restoration for years. It is worth taking a stroll along this grand old street to see the Palacio de Turismo, the pottery studio and the ACAA Gallery.

Castillo de la Real Fuerza (U/F2)

Built between 1558 and 1570, this is Havana's oldest castle. Situated at the north-eastern corner of Plaza de Armas, its restaurants and viewing terrace make it a popular meeting place. La Giradilla perched on top of the round tower has become a symbol of the city. Dating from 1631, this small bronze statue of Inés de Bobadilla looks longingly out to sea. Bobadilla took over the post of governor from her husband, Hernando de Soto, when he met a violent death in Florida in 1542.
Plaza de Armas

Castillo del Morro/Complejo Turístico Parque Histórico-Militar Morro-La Cabaña (U/E-F1)

〰️ The older part of the fortress complex is Castillo del Morro, whose tower is another of Havana's major landmarks. It was built between 1589 and 1610 to protect the town from pirate attacks. The castle was designed by the Italian military architect, Battista Antonelli, who was also responsible for planning Havana's defensive system. A military museum now occupies the site. The adjoining building, the Fortaleza de la Cabaña, was built shortly after the British withdrew in 1774. A cannon is fired every evening at 9 o'clock, as it has been for centuries, to announce the closure of the harbour. The original cannon is now kept in the Museo de la Ciudad.
At the entrance to the Bahía de la Habana; daily 09.00-21.00

Cathedral (U/F2)

Havana's cathedral serves as a reminder of the power and influence that the Catholic church

once exercised. The rapidly decaying Baroque limestone façade, now under restoration, continues to dominate the square. Built between 1748 and 1767 by Jesuits, it is home to the oldest Cuban church paintings and the tombs of former bishops. Some of the bones of Christopher Columbus, who was originally buried in Santo Domingo in the Dominican Republic, were kept here from 1796 until the end of the Spanish colonial era on Cuba in 1898 and later shipped to Seville.
Plaza de la Catedral

Necrópolis de Colón (O)

It is evident from the grandeur of the gateway that this cemetery serves as the last resting place for Havana's rich and powerful. Spaniards and revolutionaries are united here in death. Monuments and memorials recall the victims of the struggle for independence and the Revolution.
Zapata, esq. Calle 12, Vedado

Palacio de los Capitanes Generales/Museo de la Ciudad (U/F2-3)

This building is a splendid example of the grandiose style typical of Cuban palaces built at the end of the 18th century (1779-91). Massive columns dominate inside and out. Wooden boards the size of paving stones were installed as an early form of soundproofing – apparently, one of the governors complained about rattling carriages at night. It was the Spanish seat of government until 1898, then it was briefly used as the US governor's residence, and from 1902 to 1920 it was the presidential palace for the new republic. Until 1958 it

was Havana's town hall but, since its restoration in 1967, it has housed the Museo de la Ciudad (Municipal Museum). Exhibits include an array of splendid furnishings from the 18th and 19th centuries, and a marble statue of Columbus in the courtyard.
Tues-Sat 11.30-17.30, Sun 09.00-12.00; Calle Tacón, between Obispo and O'Reilly

Museum admission prices vary from $1 to $3.

Casa de África (U/F3)

An interesting display of ritual objects used by Afro-Cuban priests during religious ceremonies, many of which have been donated from private collections – Fidel Castro himself made a contribution. The museum also features a variety of exhibits from 26 different African countries.
Tues-Sat 14.30-18.30 and 19.00-21.45; Calle Obrapia 157, between Mercaderes and San Ignacio

Museo de Arte Colonial (U/F2)

This simple building, erected in 1720, was probably the first to be built near the Plaza de la Catedral and was initially inhabited by military governor Luis Chacón. The furnishings, porcelain, valuable crystal glasses and wooden panelling reflect the lifestyle of the colonial masters.
Mon and Wed-Sat 09.00-17.00, Sun 09.00-12.00; San Ignacio 61, Plaza de la Catedral

Museo Casa Natal de José Martí (U/F4)

The birthplace of poet and national hero José Martí. Displays provide some background material on his short life.

Tues-Sat 10.00-18.00, Sun 09.00-12.45; Leonor Pérez 314 between Picota and Egido

Museo Ernest Hemingway(102/C2)

Hemingway bought the Finca La Vigía in 1940 and lived there until 1960. The villa, a 20-minute drive south of the old town, has been turned into a museum. The hunting trophies, books, furniture, photos, documents and memorabilia have been kept more or less as the writer left them. The museum reopened in 1997 after extensive renovation.

Mon, Wed, Sat 09.00-16.00, Sun 09.00-12.00; Finca La Vigía, San Francisco de Paula

Museo de Historia Natural Felipe Poey

Natural history museum with displays of stuffed birds, various species of fish and shellfish, plus preserved lizards, snakes and turtles. The collection was started by the Cuban naturalist, Felipe Poey (1799-1891).

Mon-Fri 09.00-16.00; Plaza de Ignacio Agramonte, Universidad de la Habana, Edificio Felipe Poey

Museo Nacional de Artes Decorativas (O)

Chinese vases, Gobelin tapestries, ornate Rococo and Empire furniture are just some of the prized exhibits in this former residence of the Countess of Revilla de Camargo. A must for anyone with an interest in antiques.

Tues-Sat 11.00-18.30, Sun 09.00-13.00; Calle 17, esq. Calle E, Vedado

Museo Nacional de la Música (U/F4)

The museum of music houses a collection of old scores, rare and unusual instruments, records and music books. Concerts are held here to mark special occasions.

Tues-Sat 10.00-18.00, Sun 09.00-12.00; Cárcel 1, between Habana and Aguiar

Museo Nacional Palacio de Bellas Artes (U/E2)

Antiques and works by Cuban painters from the early colonial

The old presidential palace in Havana now houses the Municipal Museum

era to the present day, including some old masters (Velázquez, Goya, Rubens), are nicely presented in rather sombre rooms.
Wed-Sun 09.00-17.00; Trocadero between Zulueta and Monserrate

Museo de la Perfumería (U/F3)
Collections of famous perfumes, aromatics, soaps and mirrors in an 18th-century monastery.
Tues-Sat 14.30-21.45, Sun 09.00-13.00; Calle Oficios between Calle Obispo and Obrapia

Museo Postal Cubano (U/A5)
Alongside the first Cuban stamps dating from 1855, you can see some of the earliest telephones used on the island.
Mon-Fri 10.00-17.00; Ave. Rancho Boyeros between 19 de Mayo and 20 de Mayo, Plaza de la Revolución

Museo de la Revolución (U/E2)
Probably the most comprehensive of Cuba's many museums that document the history of the Revolution. Life-sized figures of Che Guevara and Camilo Cienfuegos portray the heroes of the guerrilla war in action.
Tues-Sat 13.00-18.00, Sun 10.00-13.00; Refugio 1, between Ave. de las Misiones and Zulueta

RESTAURANTS

1830 (O)
This white dining palace by the Malecón is one of the most elegant restaurants in Havana. Stroll from the splendid dining rooms through to the cocktail bars or on to the outdoor dance floor by the sea. Live salsa in the evenings.
Daily 12.00-23.00; Calzada 1252, Vedado, near the Miramar tunnel; Category 1-2; Tel: 07/33 45 21

Bar-Restaurant Cabaña (U/F2)
Parties are catered for downstairs, but upstairs on the roof patio the atmosphere is more intimate, with magnificent views of the Canal de Entrada and the Fortaleza de la Cabaña. Grills are prepared in front of guests. The restaurant is owned by Habaguanex S.A., which operates more than 50 restaurants, bars, cafeterias and shops in historic buildings throughout old Havana.
Daily 08.00-about 02.00; Cuba 12, esq. Peña Pobre; Category 2-3; no telephone (Habaguanex 07/33 86 93)

Café de Paris (U/F3)
Even when there are serious shortages, you should be able to get a beer or a *café cubano* here. Delightful old bar with wood-panelled walls.
Daily 12.00-19.45; Obispo 202, esq. San Ignacio; Category 3; Tel: 07/62 04 66

Castillo de Farnés (U/E3)
The waiter will be very happy to show you the table where Fidel Castro and his brother Raúl sat and ate with Che Guevara on 9 January 1959. A photo recalls the event. Intimate atmosphere, Spanish food. House speciality: prawns (*gambas*) in garlic.
Daily 12.00-24.00; Obispo/Monserrate; Category 2; Tel: 07/63 12 60

Coppelia (U/A2)
Havana's most famous ice cream parlour. Unfortunately, it only opens at irregular intervals.
Normally 10.00-24.00; Calle 23, esq. Calle L, Vedado; Category 3

Don Agamenón (O)
The blend of hi-tech lighting and flowery table decoration gives

The cathedral and Marqueses de Aguas Claras palace in the heart of old Havana

this restaurant, located in an extravagantly restored classical-style villa, a hint of modern Cuban decadence. House speciality: boiled chicken in sour orange juice with garlic and bacon.
Daily 12.00-02.00; Calle 17, no. 17, between Calle M and Calle N, Vedado; Category 2; Tel: 07/33 45 29

Dos Gardenias (O)
Modern villa, opened in 1994, which has three restaurants: one serves pizza, the other two specialize in Chinese and creole cooking. It is a popular spot with Cubans lucky enough to have the means to eat out. Video and bolero dance bar on the first floor.
Daily 12.00-02.00; 7a Ave., between Calle 2a and Calle 26, Miramar; Category 2; Tel: 07/33 23 53

El Aljibe (O)
Large restaurant with terrace near Dos Gardenias. Chicken (*pollo*), roast or fried, is the speciality here.
Daily 13.00-22.00; 7a Ave., between Calle 2a and Calle 26, Miramar; Category 2; Tel: 07/24 15 83

El Conejito (U/A2)
Small, brick-built premises sandwiched between high-rise blocks. The best place in town to sample roast rabbit.
Daily 18.00-22.00; Calle M, esq. Calle 17, Vedado; Category 2; Tel: 07/32 46 71

El Patio (U/F2)
Restaurant on the patio and in the magnificent rooms of the former palace of the Counts of Aguas Claras. The creole dishes, such as *pierna de cerdo al jugo* (leg of pork), are worth trying here. Background guitar music is often laid on.
Daily 12.00-18.30; San Ignacio, esq. Empedrado, Plaza de la Catedral; Category 2; Tel: 07/61 85 11

La Divina Pastora (U/F1-2)
Fresh fish in a romantic setting with a spectacular view of the old town. The restaurant stands directly beneath the Cabaña fortress where the 9 o'clock cannon is fired every evening to mark the closure of the harbour.
Daily 12.00-24.00; Fortaleza de la Cabaña; Category 2; Tel: 07/62 38 86

La Torre (U/A2)

◁▷ Panoramic restaurant on the 36th floor of the Fosca building (1957). The lobster is thoroughly recommended.
Daily 12.00-23.00; Calle 17, no. 55, Vedado; Category 2; Tel: 07/ 32 56 50

Las Ruinas (O)

A colourfully decked-out restaurant on the edge of Lenin Park, built around the ruined walls of an old mill, with terraces down to the park, bar and lounge.
Daily 12.00-22.00; Calle 100, esq. Cortina de la Presa, Parque Lenin; Category 1; Tel: 07/44 33 36

Papa's (O)

Fresh lobster, dance music and sea air by the Hemingway Marina.
Daily 12.00-24.00; 5a Ave. esq. Calle 248; Category 2; Tel: 07/22 55 91

SHOPPING

ACAA (U/F3)

★ Sales gallery for the Asociación Cubana de Artesanos Artistas. Cuban artists and craftworkers exhibit samples of their imaginative creations made from wood, silver, shells and papier mâché.
Daily 13.00-18.00; Obispo 411

Casa del Tabaco y
Casa del Ron (U/F3)

If cigars and rum are on your list of priorities, then this is the place to come if you want the full range to choose from.
Daily 10.00-20.00; between Obispo and Bernaza; Tel: 07/63 12 42

Diplomercado 3a y 70 (O)

Formerly a shop for diplomats, but now a supermarket where Cubans can use their dollars to buy food, meat, tinned goods, clothing and household goods.
Daily 08.00-17.00; Calle 3a, esq. Calle 70, Miramar

Palacio de la Artesanía (U/F2)

Last stop for tourist groups on the tour of the old town, where they can spend their dollars on Cuban-related paraphernalia: miniature Spanish galleons (from $39), straw hats, claves (percussion instruments made from hollow hardwood) and maracas, dolls and baskets, CDs and cassettes of Cuban music.
Daily 09.00-20.00; Cuba 64, Habana Vieja; Tel: 07/62 44 07

Palacio del Turismo (U/F3)

Souvenir shop, travel agent, tobacconist, art gallery and bar all under one roof. Sometimes used as a venue for musical events.
Obispo, esq. Cuba, Habana Vieja; Tel: 07/61 15 44

Photoservice (O)

Film laboratory (4-day developing service) and minor camera repairs.
Daily 08.00-22.00; Calle 23, esq. Calle P, Vedado; Tel: 07/33 50 31

Video Club (O)

Videos to buy and hire; CDs, Walkman cassette players and plug adaptors; plus sewing kits and fruit juices (strange but true).
Mon-Sat 10.00-21.00; Calle 3a, no. 1260, esq. Calle 14; Tel: 07/33 24 69 and 33 23 02

MARKETS

Many streets and alleys, especially around the Plaza de la Catedral, have been turned into flea markets, where handmade souvenirs, T-shirts and paintings are sold.

Mercado Agropecuario (O)

Large market building beside the Cuatro Caminos. Meat, vegetables, fruit and livestock are privately sold for Cuban pesos.
Daily 07.00-17.00

HOTELS

Ambos Mundos (U/F3)

Hemingway's first lodging place – now a family-style hotel in the pedestrian zone. The writer's old room is open to visitors. 54 rooms.
Calle E, esq. Mercaderes, Habana Vieja; Category 3; Tel: 07/66 95 30, Fax: 66 95 32

Habana Libre (U/A2)

✧ Formerly a hotel for government officials, now run by the Spanish hotel chain Tryp. Many airline offices are located here, plus the Cuban bank. Viewing terrace on the 25th floor. 568 rooms.
Between Calle L and Calle 23, Vedado; Category 1-2; Tel: 07/33 40 11, Fax: 33 31 41

Habana Riviera (O)

✧ Magnificent sea view across the Malecón. The lively atmosphere in this well-furnished hotel makes up for the rather depressing external architecture. The 'Palacio de La Salsa' is a big draw for night-owls and salsa fans (*daily from 22.00; $10*). 330 rooms.
Malecón, esq. Paseo, Vedado; Category 1-2; Tel: 07/33 40 51, Fax: 33 37 39

Hostal Valencia (U/F3)

Charming colonial-style building with 12 rooms and a patio as well as a popular bar on the second floor.
Calle Oficios 53. esq. Obrapia, Habana Vieja; Category 3; Tel: 07/ 62 38 01, Fax: 33 56 28

Inglaterra (U/E3)

This grand 19th-century hotel overlooking the palm-lined Central Park is the oldest hotel in town (1875). Immortalized in Graham Greene's novel *Our Man in Havana*, it is popular with tourists in search of nostalgia. Partly renovated in 1989, it boasts old furnishings in high-ceilinged halls, stained-glass windows and an elegant dining lounge, all now under a preservation order. Evening entertainment on the roof terrace. 83 rooms.
Paseo del Prado 416, esq. San Rafael, Habana Vieja; Category 2; Tel: 07/33 85 93-97, Fax: 33 82 54

Meliá Cohiba (O)

The high-rise hotels by the Malecón add a metropolitan touch to the Havana skyline. If you are looking for modern comfort with no expense spared, this brand new hotel is the place to stay. Cool marble, indoor fountains, swimming pool, art gallery and rooms with bath and TV. 462 rooms.
Paseo, between Calle 1a and Calle 3a, Vedado; Category 1; Tel: 07/33 36 36, Fax: 33 45 55

Nacional de Cuba (U/A2)

★ Reminiscent of an old black-and-white movie set, the dining rooms, lounges and even the lift fittings of this glamorous hotel, apparently built with mafia money, have retained that 1930s look. Recently renovated, it is regarded by many as the best hotel in town. Among the Hollywood stars who have graced its rooms are Errol Flynn, Marlon Brando and Ava Gardner. 464 rooms.
Calle O 21, Vedado; Category 1; Tel: 07/33 35 64 or 78 20 65, Fax: 33 50 54

45

Plaza (O)

This discreetly elegant hotel (1909) has just been given a facelift. Renowned for its service and comfort, it also boasts a pleasant patio cafeteria and central fountain. Excellent location for exploring the old town. A good buffet breakfast for guests and non-residents is served on the roof terrace. 188 rooms.

Ignacio Agramonte 267; Category 2; Tel: 07/33 85 83, Fax: 33 85 91/2

Residencial Turístico Marina Hemingway (O)

Two-storey building in apartment-building style at the marina. Furnished with European comforts. Surrounded by shipping canals and restaurants. Shopping centre nearby. 137 rooms.

5a Ave. and Calle 248, Santa Fe; Category 1-2; Tel: 07/24 11 50-56, Fax: 24 18 31

Sevilla (O)

Architectural tour de force from the turn of the century in the heart of Habana Vieja. Elegant ⛅ roof garden with a fine view over the old town. Inside the complex are bars and restaurants, plus sauna, massage and fitness room. 188 rooms.

Trocadero 55, between Paseo de Martí and Zulueta; Category 2; Tel: 07/33 85 60, Fax: 33 85 82

SPORTS & LEISURE

Cycling (O)

An agency named Panaciclos rents bicycles to tourists for a reasonable fee.

Ave Rancho Boyeros, esq. Santa Ana, Plaza; Tel: 07/81 01 53 and 81 41 42

Golf (O)

The Hotel Nacional de Cuba allows non-residents to use its 'Diplogolf Club' (18 holes).

Carretera de Vento, 8 km (5 mi), Reparto Capdevila, Ave. Rancho Boyeros; Tel: 07/44 48 26 and 44 82 27

Water sports

The *Hemingway Marina* at the western end of Havana (**102/B2**) is an international yachting marina. Facilities include restaurants, a disco, a shopping centre and the *Residencia Marina Hemingway*. Venue for annual deep-sea fishing competition. *Calle 48, Santa Fe Playa; Tel: 07/33 24 33.*

Cubanáutica in the *Marina Tarará* at the start of the *Playas del Este* (**102/C2**) charters yachts for the day, organizes boat excursions, fishing trips and diving expeditions. *Paseo 309, between Calle 13 and Calle 15, Plaza de la Revolución; Tel: 07/33 45 46/7, Fax: 33 45 45.*

BEACHES

Playas del Este (102/C2-103/D2)

The coastal stretch to the east of Havana is lined with popular beaches, one of the most beautiful of which is the Playa Megano (23 km/14 mi) overlooked by the *Horizontes Villa Megano Resort, Vía Blanca (198 rooms; Category 2; Tel: 07/97 16 10, Fax: 97 16 24).* Next door is the Playa Santa María with the informal *Tropicoco Beach Club (188 rooms; between Ave. Sur and Ave. de las Terrazas; Category 3; Tel: 07/33 80 40 or 0687/25 31, Fax: 33 51 56).*

The long promenade is lined with small restaurants and food stalls and the *Finca El Palmar* by Playa Guanabo further east is often used as a venue for Afro-Cuban musical events.

There is a total of eight beaches on the Playas del Este stretch. Five of them are situated close to one another: Bacuranao, Megano, Santa María, Boca Ciega and Guanabo. Jibacoa, El Abra and Trópico lie some 60 km (40 mi) east of Havana.

ENTERTAINMENT

Cabaret Tropicana   (O)
Internationally renowned dance show full of glitz and glamour. The Afro-Cuban performance is particularly rousing. After the show, the band carries on playing for anyone who wants to dance.
Tues-Sun 21.00-02.00; admission: $50; between Calle 72 and Calle 43, no. 4504, Marianao; Tel: 07/20 51 44 and 20 42 15

El Floridita   (U/F2)
'My *mojito* in the Bodeguita, my daiquiri in the Floridita.' That was how Hemingway whiled away his evenings, together with artists, intellectuals and politicians. Apparently the ever-thirsty writer always sat on the first bar stool in the Floridita. Fresh fish and lobsters feature among the recommended dishes served in the small adjoining restaurant.
Daily 12.00-01.00; Obispo, esq. Monserrate, Habana Vieja; Category 1-2; Tel: 07/63 11 11 and 63 10 63

La Bodeguita del Medio   (U/F2)
✪ The second of Hemingway's favourite watering holes is now permanently full of tourists who come here to sample his favourite cocktail. Made with rum, lemon juice, fresh mint and soda, the *mojito* is mixed to perfection here.
Empedrado 207, Habana Vieja; Tel: 07/62 44 98 and 61 84 42

La Maison   (O)
An evening haunt often frequented by tourist groups, who are served a blend of Cuban live music and sophisticated fashion parades.
Daily 20.00-02.00; Calle 16, no. 701, esq. 7a Ave., Miramar; Tel: 07/ 33 15 43 and 33 15 48

Palacio de la Salsa   (O)
Havana's top night spot. Live salsa bands and dancing every night from 22.00.
admission: $10; Hotel Habana Riviera, Malecón, esq. Paseo, Vedado, entrance Calle 1a; Tel: 07/30 90 91

Teatro García Lorca   (U/E3)
Cuba's national ballet company performs behind the cluttered Baroque and neo-classical façade of this splendid theatre (1838). Poetry readings are also held here. The auditorium seats up to 2000 spectators.
Between Paseo del Prado and San Rafael; Tel: 07/61 30 78

INFORMATION

Cubanacán (Hotels), Calle 23, between 15a and 17, Reparto Siboney; Tel: 07/33 60 06, Fax: 33 60 46, e-mail: aloja@pradera.cha.cyt.cu
Cubatur, Calle 23, no. 156, Vedado, Ciudad de la Habana, Cuba; Tel: 07/ 33 41 55-60, Fax: 33 41 14

SURROUNDING AREA

Cayo Levisa   (101/E2)
Tiny island in the Los Colorados archipelago off the north coast of Pinar del Río province. Excursions are offered from Havana. The *Cayo Levisa*, a cabaña hotel (*20 rooms; Category 2*), provides accommodation.

Cojímar (102/C2)

A large bar, colourfully decorated tables, photos of Ernest Hemingway on the walls and a magnificent view of the sea, which was the inspiration for the American writer's masterpiece *The Old Man and the Sea*. The bar called *La Terraza* in this fishing village, a 20-minute drive from Havana, seems to reflect Hemingway's personality more than any other bar in Havana. Fresh fish is, of course, the restaurant's speciality. Try *mariscor* (a whole fish – depending on the day's catch – in a 'salt mantle'). The bar prides itself on its wide range of cocktails.

Daily 12.00-22.30; Calle Real 161 between Montaña and Candelaria; Category 2; Tel: 07/65 34 71

Guanabacoa (102/C2)

The Museo Histórico de Guanabacoa, arguably the most interesting museum of the Santoría cult, is situated in the north-east of Havana (*Mon, Wed-Sat 10.30-18.00, Sun 09.00-13.00; José Martí 108, between Versalles and San Antonio; Tel: 07/ 90 91 17*). Many of the exhibits are ritual objects used by some of the main religious sects: the Santoría, the Regla de Ocha (or Regla de Palo or Palo-Monte) and the Sociedad Secreta Abakua.

Isla de la Juventud (104/A-C 3-5)

Shipwrecks off the coast, pirate legends and a real treasure hoard help to cultivate the belief that this island, formerly known as Isla de Pinos (Pine Island), was the inspiration for Robert Louis Stevenson's *Treasure Island*.

Fidel Castro was also incarcerated here. He was sent to the Presidio Modelo, now the *Museo Nacional de la Historia*, in the main town of Nueva Gerona (*Mon-Sat 10.00-18.00, Sun 10.00-15.00*) after his failed attack on the Moncada barracks in Santiago de Cuba in 1953. He later renamed the island Isla de la Juventud – the Isle of Youth – a name that honours its promise. The island is now the base for some 50 schools and education camps (Escuelas Básicas en el Campo), where thousands of students from the countries Cuba has forged relations with come to study languages, history and geography. They liven up the town of Nueva Gerona (pop. 33,000), the tropical fruit plantations and, in their leisure time, the otherwise quiet ⚓ beaches. The finest beach, about 15 km (10 mi) long, is found 60 km (40 mi) south of the town.

The island's main hotel is situated near the *Carretera de Siguenea*. The *Hotel Colony* is very popular with scuba divers as over 50 deep-water diving sites are located nearby. You can hire equipment and take lessons if you want to explore the underwater reefs and shipwrecks. Other activities include tennis, horseback riding and surfing (*77 rooms; Category 2; Tel: 982 82 and 981 81*).

Air Cubana operates several daily flights to the Isla de la Juventud from Havana. The island does not usually feature on the itinerary of tour operators.

Near the Museo Nacional in Nueva Gerona is the *Museo Finca El Abra (Tues-Sun 09.00-17.00; Carretera Siguenea, 2 km/1.2 mi)*, which is definitely worth a visit. Cuba's national hero José Martí was held prisoner here.

The fascinating diving grounds off the wonderful beaches of the Isla de la Juventud are a major tourist attraction

Madruga (103/D3)

The main attraction is the *Museo Etnográfico.* Formerly a temple for Afro-Cuban ceremonies, it now houses many of the priests' ritual objects (*daily 09.00-17.00; admission $1*).

Pinar del Río (101/E3)

Pinar del Río is a small, but busy, town, and yet it is hard to believe that it is home to about 100,000 people. Calle Martí, the main thoroughfare lined with low colonnaded houses, is a remnant of the prosperous plantation days when tobacco planters took advantage of the fertile soil in the surrounding area and brought great wealth to the town. The tobacco that is cultivated here is said to be the best in the world. Planters continue to live and work here, often independently.

The most impressive houses are found right on the main street José Martí, among them the *Teatro Milanés* which first opened in 1845 and was named in honour of the Cuban poet José Jacinto Milanés. The *Museo Histórico Pinares* next door provides a wide range of interesting historical information (*Tues-Sun 10.00-12.00 and 13.00-18.00*).

The principal attraction, however, is the tobacco factory *Francisco Donatien*, easily identifiable from afar by its fresh coat of paint. Visitors are always welcome, although they may feel rather like intruders at a family gathering.

Watching the *tabaqueros* at work is, nevertheless, a fascinating experience. The factory has a small souvenir shop and a museum (*Mon-Fri 08.00-17.00*).

There are few good hotels in Pinar del Río. The *Horizontes La Ermita* is one of the better ones (*62 rooms; Carretera de la Ermita; 2 km/1½ mi; Category 3; Tel: 0829/ 32 04*).

Soroa (102/A3)

The gently undulating region between Havana and Pinar del Río is centred around the town of Soroa. This area has been declared a biosphere reserve by UNESCO. An interesting site to visit here is the *Orquideario*, a botanical garden with over 350 different species of orchid. Blossoming season is from November to April. The guided tour takes about 20 minutes. The nearby waterfall is a great place for a cool, refreshing shower.

From the top of the *Mirador de Venus* (a half-hour climb) one can enjoy a spectacular view. A short path (500 m) leads from the gardens to the *El Salto* waterfall dropping 22 m (70 ft) into a rock basin.

Hotel recommendation: *Horizontes Villa Soroa; 49 bungalows; Carretera de Soroa; 8 km/5 mi; Category 3; Tel: 082/21 22.*

VARADERO

(103/F2) Advertising hoardings, freshly-painted façades and tourists on mopeds or in flashy hired jeeps in Varadero (pop. 12,000) let one forget communism. The name of this elongated peninsula of Hicaco, about two hours' drive from Havana, is for many a synonym for the new Cuba. Its airport, the second-largest on Cuba, receives most of the charter flights from Spain, Italy, Canada, Germany and the UK.

Hicaco came to prominence at around the turn of the century when wealthy Cubans and Americans built weekend homes

---

Hemingway's struggle

Born on 21 July 1899 in Oak Park, Illinois, Hemingway chose Cuba as his home. He first came here in 1928 and was captivated. He returned in 1932 and stayed until 1961. The underlying theme of his writing is man's (and his own) conflict with nature. He often portrays machismo, but coupled with a sense of social commitment. Pride and honour, victory and defeat are other recurring themes in his work. They can be clearly identified in his novel The Old Man and the Sea, in which he describes a fisherman's physical and mental struggle as he hauls in a large fish. This work won him the Pulitzer Prize in 1953 and the Nobel Prize for literature in 1954. The inspiration for it came from the many fishing expeditions he embarked on from Cojímar near Havana. Always championing the fighter and increasingly those struggling for greater social justice, he welcomed Castro's Revolution and remained on Cuba. But the constant struggle within himself eventually took its toll. As he grew older he found writing increasingly difficult. Nineteen days before his 62nd birthday, Hemingway shot himself while on a hunting expedition in Ketchum, Idaho.

here. They went on to organize sailing regattas and to open casinos, while the local people were denied access to the beach. The Revolution brought an end to these wealthy pursuits, and Varadero stagnated as a holiday resort, although the Cuban government did enact a law 'proclaiming the people's full right to enjoy the beaches'. When the USSR collapsed, the Cuban authorities needed to attract large-scale tourism from capitalist countries to boost the flagging economy, and looked immediately to Varadero. It is now a well-established beach resort almost on a par with Miami, but many Cubans are ambivalent about its new status. Ironically, the situation has almost turned full circle. The new developments are the preserve of the foreign holidaymakers staying in dollar hotels, and the region is losing some of its Cuban character; some might even argue that Varadero is an ideal place to holiday if you do not want to meet any Cubans apart from the staff who look after the tourists. Foreign hotel firms pay the Cuban government on average $400 a month per employee. The government keeps the dollars and pays the workers in nearly worthless pesos. The main bonuses for the workers are the hard currency tips, and the access to good food. Long before the advent of tourism, the peninsula was home to a small fishing community and it was also covered by salt flats that supplied all of Cuba with salt. Now Varadero takes up virtually the whole of the peninsula, which extends for about 18 km or 12 miles. A light, pleasant breeze always blows off the sea.

What must be the finest beach in Cuba runs for about 12 km (7½ mi) along the north side of the peninsula. It consists of fine-grained coral sand, which glows a milky turquoise colour beneath the gentle (and very safe) sea.

SIGHTS

Cueva de Ambrosio
Caves beside the Autopista Sur, where some interesting ancient Indian cave drawings have been found.

Retiro Josone
❂ Well-maintained park with white geese and a small, artificial lake. Footpaths, giant *ceiba* trees, two garden cafés, three restaurants and cycle hire.
1a Ave., esq. Calle 57

MUSEUMS

Museo Municipal
The municipal museum, set in an attractive wooden, turn-of-the-century house, documents the development of Varadero. Look out for the stones with Indian engravings in the garden.
Mon-Sat 10.00-19.00, Sun 14.00-18.00; between Ave. Playa and Calle 57

Villa DuPont
Built in the late 1920s as a holiday home for the French chemicals magnate Eleuthère Irénée Du-Pont, Xanadú cost $338,000 to build, although the land was virtually free. This lavish mansion is still standing today and is one of the few genuine tourist attractions in Varadero. The mahogany ceilings and the staircase that leads up to the living and sleeping

Stone sculpture on the golf course at the former DuPont estate

quarters are all original. The marble baths with their priceless Art Nouveau and Art Deco fittings are worth a closer look.
Daily 12.00-23.00; Ave. Las Américas

RESTAURANTS

Antigüedades
Plush decor with lace tablecloths, Moorish figures and gilded picture frames in a pavilion in Josone Park. The proprietress welcomes guests in creole dress. Fish soup is her speciality.
Daily from 18.00; 1a Ave./Retiro Josone; Category 1

Casa de Al Capone
This extravagantly furnished house with its Portuguese tiles and fireplace was built in 1934 and allegedly financed by the mafia. At one time it was owned by the notorious Chicago gangster Al Capone. Today it is one of the best restaurants on the southern tip of the Hicaco peninsula. Recommendations include the *bocaditas* (sandwiches), tortillas and the fish dishes.
Daily 09.00-01.00; Ave. Kawama; Category 1-2; Tel: 05/639 16-244

El Barajeque
Seafood restaurant in a wooden cabin. Be sure to sample the *mojo criollo*, a spicy sauce served with grilled fish.
Daily 12.00-24.00; Calle O, esq. Camino del Mar; Complejo Turístico Kawama; Category 2

Istmo

Pleasant restaurant by the Hotel Dos Mares. Standard dishes include *pescado del día* (fish of the day) and *arroz moro* (black beans and rice) with grilled meat.
Daily 12.00-22.00; 1a Ave., esq. Calle 53; Category 2; Tel: 05/627 02

Las Américas

〰️ Dine out in opulent surroundings at the famous DuPont villa. French specialities are served on colourfully decorated tables beneath a mahogany beam ceiling or out on the sea-view terrace.
Daily 10.00-23.00; Ave. Las Américas; Category 1; Tel: 05/662 38

Mallorca

This restaurant, situated at the entrance to the Centro Comercial El Caimán, has a few chairs outside, a bar for quick service and a small neatly furnished restaurant inside. Specialities include paella, fish and chicken.
Daily 12.00-24.00; 1a Ave., esq. Calle 71; Category 2; Tel: 05/631 03

Mesón

Langosta a la Habana is the speciality of this pretty Retiro Josone garden villa. The creole dishes are also worth trying.
Daily 12.30-23.00; 1a Ave., esq. Calle 54; Category 1; Tel: 05/629 33

Mesón del Quijote

This restaurant enjoys a romantic setting next to an old windmill, which is illuminated at night. It specializes in Spanish fare – the seafood paella is especially good. You will be serenaded by guitar music while you eat.
Daily 15.00-23.00; Villa Cuba; Category 1-2; Tel: 05/635 22 and 629 75

Steak House

A grill restaurant in an old villa. While the meat is cooking on the spit, you can sit on the terrace listening to musicians performing Cuban songs and watch the horse-drawn carts trot by with their tourist passengers. Aside from beef, the restaurant also serves grilled fish, lobster, prawns and chicken. If you have any special requests, you should let the chef know the day before. Groups, friends and families can use the lounge and the terrace on the first floor.
Daily 12.00-24.00; 1a Ave., esq. Calle 73; Category 1-2; Tel: 05/634 35

SHOPPING

Many of the formerly coop-run souvenir and bookshops in Varadero have recently been half-privatized or transformed into new state-owned businesses competing in the marketplace much like private firms. Accordingly, one should not be surprised if shop names continue to change. In general, however, the opening times given on page 29 also apply to the shops listed here.

Boutique Arte Nuevo

Well-stocked souvenir stand near the ageing Copey hotels. The jewellery, much of it made from silver, coral and shells, is especially pretty.
2a Ave., esq. Calle 64

Casa de Latin Arte

Handicrafts from Latin American countries like Ecuador, Venezuela and Guatemala. Clay figures, calabash bowls, dolls, materials and painted wooden plates.
1a Ave., esq. Calle 73

Centro Comercial El Caimán

Park with shopping villas, the small Mallorca restaurant, a photo developing service, a boutique and plenty of souvenirs. After a wander round the shops, for about $3 you can catch a ride home in one of the horse-drawn carts that wait here.

3a Ave., esq. Calle 63

Reproducciones Artistas Publicitarias

Handcrafted souvenirs such as stuffed dolls and sisal tapestries. Look out for the large, crocheted tablecloths.

1a Ave., esq. Calle 44

Retiro Josone

A young and gifted amateur artist, Nelson Castro, sells his paintings beside the park entrance.

1a Ave., between Calle 56 and Calle 59

Taller de Cerámica Artistas

Sales gallery and studio of Cuban potters. The artists here set high standards. No kitsch, no mass production, just classical and imaginative designs.

1a Ave., behind the Hotel Atabey

HOTELS

Barlovento

Architecturally diverse holiday hotel complex in a central spot about 100 m (330 ft) from the beach. Good atmosphere and ideal for families. 271 rooms.

1a Ave., between Calle 10 and Calle 12; Category 1; Tel: 05/66 71 40, Fax: 66 72 18

Bella Costa LTI

★ Every room has a sea view, minibar and cable TV. Breakfast includes a selection of bread rolls and different types of bread. Events are organized in the evening in the pool bar and there's a disco. 307 rooms.

Ave. Las Américas; Category 1; Tel: 05/66 75 22, Fax: 66 74 75

Complejo Internacional

Now under the new management of the Gran Caribe chain and recently given a facelift, this hotel, right on the beach, offers every luxury: a stately approach, a tropical garden and an entertainment programme called 'Cabaret Continental'. 319 rooms.

Ave. Las Américas; Category 1; Tel: 05/66 70 38, Fax: 66 72 46

Cuatro Palmas

Falls somewhere between an urban business hotel and a holiday hotel. Built around a small swimming pool in a tropical garden setting. Restaurant and bar; well-maintained, clean and centrally located. 343 rooms.

1a Ave., esq. Calle 62; Category 1; Tel: 05/66 70 40, Fax: 66 72 08

Dos Mares

Small, family-run hotel with bright, spotlessly clean and recently renovated rooms. Central location, only three minutes from the beach. 32 rooms.

1a Ave., esq. Calle 53; Category 3; Tel: 05/627 02

Meliá

Waterfalls in the bright lobby, glass lifts sliding noiselessly up and down above the bamboos growing in the inner courtyard: a first-class hotel, which does justice to the excellent reputation of this South American hotel chain. 490 rooms.

Fidel Castro on 1 May 1994:

El mundo está en manos de los capitalistas, y una revolución tan pura y firme como la nuestra está obligada a tomar en cuenta esta realidad. – The world is in the hands of the capitalists, and a revolution as pure and as strong as ours has to take this reality into account.

Autopista Sur, Playa de las Américas; Category 1; Tel: 05/662 20-29, Fax: 33 70 11

Paradiso-Puntarena

Two holiday hotels belonging to the Spanish Tryp chain. Lagoon-style swimming pool complex with lots of greenery. Shared beach and restaurant facilities. Fun-loving, casual atmosphere. Good range of sports facilities. 512 rooms (both hotels).
Between Ave. Kawama and Calle Final; Category 1-2; Tel: 05/66 71 20, Fax: 66 70 74

Pullman

'Simple and central' is how this small hotel with the neo-Gothic tower promotes itself – modest claims which are easily met. Value for money is the key. Relaxing restaurant with a comfortable bar. 15 rooms.
1a Ave., between Calle 49 and Calle 50; Category 3; Tel: 05/625 75

Resort Kawama

An extensive holiday complex, consisting of detached villas adjacent to the beach. A peaceful hideaway for singles, groups or families. The Gran Caribe chain has improved facilities and the complex now boasts a children's pool, five restaurants serving different cuisines, five bars and a disco. 312 rooms.
Calle O, Camino del Mar; Category 1/2; Tel: 05/66 71 56, Fax: 66 70 04

Ríu-Las Morlas

Opened in 1993, this well-maintained hotel is for the perfectionist. Competent staff at reception, flowers in the pool garden, pleasant furnishings. 148 rooms.
Ave. Las Américas; Category 2; Tel: 05/639 13, Fax: 66 70 07

Sol Palmeras

This complex blends in well with the surroundings. The terraced apartment blocks are built around a swimming pool. Uncomplicated and ideal for children. Set out of the way at the tip of the Hicaco peninsula. 439 rooms.
Carretera Las Morlas, Playa de las Américas; Category 1; Tel: 05/66 70 09, Fax: 66 70 08

Tuxpan LTI

Not much older than the neighbouring Bella Costa. Highlights of this first-class holiday hotel include the excellent El Rancho restaurant and Cuba's top disco, La Bamba. 233 rooms.
Ave. Las Américas; Category 1; Tel: 05/66 75 60, Fax: 66 72 05

SPORTS & LEISURE

Diving

Tuxpan LTI, Paradiso-Puntarena and Sol Palmeras offer diving lessons. Otherwise contact the Barracuda diving school through your hotel (for certificate courses go to *1a Ave., between Calle 55 and Calle 56*)

Parachute jumping

Varadero is one of the few places in the Caribbean that has a parachute jumping centre. The MI-8 helicopters can carry up to 18 passengers. For information about prices, enquire at the *Centro Internacional de Paracaidismo, Vía Blanca; 1.5 km/1 mi; Tel: 037/ 33 70 61, Fax: 33 70 62*

Riding

If you would like to explore the surrounding countryside on horseback, book your ride at one of the following hotels: *Tuxpan LTI, Bella Costa LTI, Cuatro Palmas or Sol Palmeras*

Sailing

Amateur sailors can make use of three yachting marinas: *Acua, Gaviota and Chapelín*

Surfing

Board hire from the *Internacional Hotel*

Tennis

The *Tuxpan LTI* and *Meliá* hotels both have tennis courts

Varadero Golf Club Cuba

This wonderfully situated 18-hole golf course has recently been expanded to full size.
Tel: 07/66 21 13, Fax: 33 41 94

Varasub

A Japanese submarine that holds up to 48 passengers takes tourists on underwater excursions from Punta Blanca Villa on the outskirts of Varadero. It usually does six trips a day. Fare: adults $35, children $20. Reservations can be made through *Tour and Travel, Ave. Playa 3606, between Calle 36 and Calle 37; Tel: 05/637 13*

Water sports

The water sports school *Surf & Sail* (*VDWS*) rents out Topcat catamarans, surfboards, jet bikes and pedalos. The school also offers lessons in sailing and surfing. *Further information from the stands outside the Internacional and Tuxpan LTI hotels*

ENTERTAINMENT

Amfiteatro

Open-air theatre that stages regular performances and events, including guest dance ensembles and theatre groups. Every hotel will have full programme details. *Wed-Mon from 09.00; esq. Vía Blanca/Autopista Sur*

Cabaret Continental

A smaller and somewhat more authentic 'Tropicana Show' to be enjoyed American style over a formal dinner; *Hotel Varadero Internacional, Carretera Las Américas, Tel. 05/66 70 38, Tickets $25 ($40 with dinner)*

Cueva La Pirata

Cave converted into a disco and bar; room for about 200 people. *Mon-Sat 21.00-03.00; just off the Ave. Las Américas, behind the Hotel Sol Palmeras; Tel: 05/632 24*

El Kastillito

⚱ A roof made from palm leaves helps to absorb the noise emanating from this popular disco. Young Cubans mix with the tourists to the sound of son and pop. *Daily 21.00-03.00; Ave. Playa, esq. Calle 49*

La Bamba

❖ Sexily-dressed Cuban girls often mill around outside in the hope of gaining entry as a companion. Westerners will feel at home in this flash disco. The Cubans love it too. (*22.00-03.00; in the Hotel Tuxpan LTI*)

La Patana
Disco on a barge that has lost out to the big hotel discos, which means it is less crowded. The rhythms are mainly Cuban.
Daily 21.00-03.00; near the Vía Blanca quay

SURROUNDING AREA

Cárdenas   (106/A1-2)
This 'town of horse-drawn carts' where the first Cuban flag was hoisted in 1850 is situated about 18 km (12 mi) east of Varadero. No need to worry about petrol rationing here; the best way to explore Cárdenas (pop. 70,000) is in one of the horse-drawn carriages, which ferry both tourists and locals around. Bicycles and carts far outnumber motorized transport. One of the town's focal points is the Parque Colón, where the island's first memorial to Christopher Columbus stands. The *Museo Oscar María de Rojas* was one of Cuba's first museums (*Tues-Sat 13.00-18.00, Sun 09.00-13.00; Calzada 4*). Its prized exhibit is a splendidly decorated 19th-century coach which looks like a royal theatre box on wheels.

Cayo Largo   (105/F4-5)
The island of Cayo Largo (38 sq km/15 sq mi) is less than an hour from Varadero by plane. This holiday playground off the south coast is set in beautifully clear Caribbean waters and is blessed with a 25 km (15½ mi) snow-white stretch of sand along its southern coast. The best beach is the 2 km (1½ mi) long *Playa Sirena* which offers not only great swim-

Catamarans for hire on the beach near Varadero

ming but also a centre for water sports, a restaurant and shops. Cayo Largo has been a tourist destination for many years now. Even if you are staying on mainland Cuba, it's worth considering one of the organized excursions from Havana. If you're interested in snorkelling, catamaran sailing or scuba-diving contact *Cubanáutica*. Four hotel complexes are promoted under the name *Isla del Sur Resort*, and all are run by the Gran Caribe hotel chain: the *Isla del Sur resort (112 rooms; split into two smaller sites); Villa Coral (60 rooms; in a neo-colonial holiday village); Villa Iguana (114 rooms)*; and the cosy *Cabañas Capricho (60 thatched bungalows)*. All of the above are situated beside the magnificent white coral sand beach *(Isla del Sur Resort, Cayo Largo del Sur, Archipiélago de los Canarreos; Category 2; Tel: 095/2104-07, Fax: 2104-08)*.

Until the new airport building is finished, the old one is still being used as departure lounge by day and turns into the *Blue Lake* disco by night.

Ciénaga de Zapata (106/A4-5)

Nature-lovers should not miss an excursion to this protected wetland area (tours depart from Havana, Varadero and Cienfuegos). The Montemar Nature Park extends the full length of the peninsula and most of it can be viewed from a boat. Dense mangrove forest vegetation provides the perfect habitat for unusual aquatic birds, and rare wild lilies and aquatic plants thrive in the wet climate. Make sure you are equipped with mosquito repellent. The *Fiesta Campesino (creole cuisine; daily 08.00-18.00; Tel: 059/20 45)* by the Carretera Australia access road is worth a visit.

The unique Botica Francesa pharmaceutical museum in Matanzas

A small zoo shelters animals of the Ciénaga de Zapata.

The gateway to this huge area is *La Boca* by the *Laguna del Tesoro*. Thatched open-air restaurants, landing stages and a pottery workshop surround the large car park, which always seems to be packed with tourist coaches. You can visit the crocodile farm here and even sample a crocodile steak if you are feeling adventurous.

The main destination of the boat trips from La Boca (by either speed boat or large, slower tourist vessels) is the Indian village of *Guamá*, where some 32 life-sized sculptures by the artist Rita Longa seek to convey an impression of the Siboney Indian way of life. Overnight accommodation is available in comfortable wooden cabins (*Horizontes Villa Guamá, Laguna del Tesoro; 50 rooms; Category 3; Tel: 059/29 79*).

The *Bahía de Cochinos*, better known as the Bay of Pigs, cuts inland towards La Boca. There are two simple bungalow hotel complexes by the bay: the palm-shaded *Playa Larga* (*Horizontes Playa Larga; Category 3; Tel: 07/ 33 75 42 and 059/72 94, Fax: 059/41 41*) and the *Horizontes Playa Girón* (*Category 3; Tel: 0733/75 28 and 059/41 18*). Facilities at the latter include restaurants, a bar, a disco, car hire and stables.

The *Playa Girón* lies further south. It was here in 1961 that Cuban exiles landed in the mistaken belief that the country needed help in freeing itself from communism. An old fighter plane, the *Museo de la Intervención (Tues-Sun 09.00-17.00)*, and 48 stone memorial tablets (by the access road) recall the unsuccessful incursion.

Matanzas (103/E2)

Once the principal sugar-exporting port, the capital of Matanzas province (pop. 100,000), is today one of Cuba's main industrial centres. No more than a half-hour's drive away from Varadero, there are some interesting sights to see in and around the historic centre. One of the town's best attractions is the ★ *Botica Francesa* by the Parque Libertad. Originally a chemist's shop founded in 1882, it now houses a unique pharmaceutical museum. Everything has been kept almost exactly as the last owner left it: the high prescription counter, the giant potion jars, the ancient medical instruments and Cuba's oldest refrigerator which stands in the chemist's kitchen (*Parque de la Libertad/Calle Maceo; Mon-Sat 10.00-18.00, Sun 09.00-13.00*). If you walk a little further down the Calle Maceo towards the harbour, you will come to the grand neoclassical *Teatro Sauto* (1862), an impressive reminder of Matanzas' heyday as the cultural centre of Cuba. The best view of Matanzas and the surrounding countryside can be seen from the ruins of the Iglesia de Monserrate, in the hills to the north of the town centre.

One of the most popular tourist attractions in the area is the *Bellamar Caves* 5 km (about 3 miles) south of the town. Discovered in 1961, these caves, 2 km (1½ miles) long, have some fine stalactites and stalagmites. They are also noted for the remains of some prehistoric mammals that were found among the rubble. To visit them join one of the organized excursions, as the cave entrance is not always manned.

Quaint historic towns and coral islands

Lively resorts against a backdrop of rural tradition

The heart of Cuba serves as a sort of buffer zone between cosmopolitan Havana in the west and the Caribbean atmosphere of Santiago de Cuba in the east. The people of this peaceful and rural area with the Escambray Mountains to the south are easy-going and firmly rooted in tradition. This was where, in 1958, Che Guevara went on the offensive against government troops and captured the town of Santa Clara, the first conquest for the revolutionary army. Reservoirs and wide stretches of water lend the mountain landscape a slightly melancholy air, but this soon dissipates when you reach the southern Caribbean coast where you will discover two of Cuba's loveliest towns. Cienfuegos, with its newly renovated central area and the popular Bohemian Punta Gorda quarter, is full of old world charm. One hour's drive south of Cienfuegos, set inland on a hill, is the splendid colonial town of

Trinidad. Here the faded splendour of church towers and aristocratic mansions hark back to the prosperous days of the sugar boom at the beginning of the 19th century. Continue south on the Carretera Central and you will come to another colonial gem of a town: Camagüey, the 'golden heart' and third largest town in Cuba, is a lively blend of past and present.

Those in search of peace and relaxation can take refuge in the islands off the north coast. The long Archipiélago de Camagüey is linked to the mainland by a land bridge. It is made up of countless tiny *cayos*, coral islands with snow-white beaches, that lie like links in a chain, surrounded by reefs, in the crystal-clear waters south-east of the Bahamas. This region is a haven for snorkellers, divers, and deep-sea fishing enthusiasts. Most tourists head for the linked islands of Cayo Coco and Cayo Guillermo, a large expanse of land with a proliferation of resort developments. If you want to meet more locals, the resort of Playa Santa Lucía on the mainland is popular with Cubans.

The Palacio de Valle in Cienfuegos, built in classical Moorish Gothic style, dates from 1913

CAMAGÜEY

(111/F3) Despite its size (pop. ca. 300,000), this town in the heart of Cuba exudes the charm of an old, provincial capital with a long history. Its symbol is the *tinajón*, a large, wide-mouthed earthenware jug, modelled on the big-bellied jars that were brought over from Spain filled with wines and oils. Here, however, it was used for storing rainwater. Founded in 1515 by Diego de Velázquez, Camagüey was originally situated on the coast near Nuevitas and was known as Santa María Puerto Príncipe, but it was later relocated inland away from the inhospitable marshy terrain. It was renamed after an Indian chief (*cazique*) called Camagüey who lived here in the time of Christopher Columbus. Prosperity was brought to the region by Spanish aristocrats from Toledo who grew sugar cane and raised cattle on the flat pastures. Their wealth is reflected in the architecture of the old town. It is a web of turns and culs-de-sac, dotted with churches that have survived the centuries almost unscathed. These are now under preservation order.

The best way to explore Camagüey is by horse and cart, which for many inhabitants has replaced the car. You can even enter the old theatre on horseback just as the townsfolk did over 100 years ago. The production may well be a performance by the Ballet de Camagüey, a company founded in 1967 which is now regarded as Cuba's second-best troupe (after the National Ballet in Havana). Several of the town's citizens have contributed to its reputation as a cultural centre: Carlos F. Finlay (1833-1915) discovered the antidote to yellow fever, Ignacio Agramonte was a heroic general in the first War of Independence, and Nicolás Guillén, a famous poet.

Camagüey is one of the stations on the Havana to Santiago de Cuba railway line. Prior to train departures, the station in the town centre is buzzing with human activity.

SIGHTS

Parque Agramonte

🏃 Boards giving botanical information have been affixed to some of the trees, which also provide generous shade in this popular

MARCO POLO SELECTION: THE CENTRE

1 Cayo Coco
The perfect tropical paradise with white coral beaches and luxurious hotels (page 65)

2 Hanabanilla Reservoir
A picturesque artificial lake nestling in the mountains, amid a wonderfully tranquil landscape (page 71)

3 Museo Romántico in Trinidad
A charming aristocratic mansion stuffed with fine furnishings and other colonial treasures (page 70)

4 Palacio de Valle in Cienfuegos
Enjoy fresh lobster while admiring the Moorish mosaics and alabaster (page 64)

park. Attractions include goat-drawn carts for children, a youth centre with swimming pool and disco, a concert arena and a small zoo whose star attraction is Pancho the lion.

Plaza San Juan de Dios

Surrounded by grand merchants' houses, restaurants and the Church of San Juan de Dios, this is one of the town's finest colonial squares. A flea market with food stalls is held here every evening from 8 o'clock.

MUSEUMS

Casa Natal Ignacio Agramonte

Birthplace of the heroic general, Ignacio Agramonte, who died in the battle of Las Guasimas in 1873, and was one of Cuba's greatest patriots. His favourite ploy in battle was to feign retreat, lure the enemy into a false sense of security, then strike.
Tues-Sun 09.00-13.00; between Agramonte and Candelaria; admission: $1

Museo Provincial de Historia Ignacio Agramonte

Former Spanish barracks with a large, shady, inner courtyard. The high-ceilinged rooms contain exhibits relating to natural and local history and paintings.
Tues-Sun 09.00-17.00; Ave. Mártires; admission: $1

RESTAURANTS

El Orejito

Small patio and separate bar in a former Spanish mansion still furnished with antiques. Specializes in meat dishes.
Daily 10.00-22.00; Hermanos Agüero 280; Category 2; Tel: 0322/952 24

La Campana de Toledo

Formerly a merchant's house. Red stone floor and a patio filled with palms, royal poinciana and almond trees. Specializes in pork dishes.
Daily 10.00-18.00; Plaza San Juan de Dios; Category 3; Tel: 0322/958 88

SHOPPING

Atelier Oscar Rodríguez La Seria

This Cuban artist of international renown sells tasteful ceramics from his own studio. Advance notice required.
Bellavista 420; Tel: 0322/814 16

HOTELS

Horizontes Camagüey

Old-world hotel belonging to the Cuban Horizonte hotel chain. 142 rooms.
Carretera Central; 4.5 km/3 mi, Este; Category 3; Tel: 0322/720 15, Fax: 33 99 56

Maraguán

Hacienda-style hotel on a breezy hill to the east of the town. Restaurants, pool, shops, playground and open-air disco. 35 rooms.
Circunvalación Este; Category 2-3; Tel: 0322/720 17 and 721 70

Plaza

Colonial-style hotel with simple furnishings, opposite the station. The rooms overlooking the inner courtyard are quieter. 67 rooms.
Van Horne 1; Category 3; Tel: 0322/824 35

ENTERTAINMENT

Bar El Cambio

This simple corner bar decorated by Oscar Rodríguez La Seria is a popular meeting place for local intellectuals.

Daily 00.00-24.00; Martí 152; no telephone

Casa de Trova

Live bands play Cuban songs on the historic patio on Saturday and Sunday from 9 pm.

Martí y Cristo 171; Tel: 0322/913 57

El Cartel

The walls of this bar are plastered with old film posters, copies of which are for sale.

Daily 09.00-17.00; Cisneros 208, between Martí and Hermanos Agüero

Teatro Principal

Built in 1850, this fine old theatre has been restored and now stages some interesting productions, with regular performances by the local ballet company.

General Espinosa; admission: $3

CIENFUEGOS

(106/C4-5) The magnificently restored main square with theatre, pavilion and rows of seating for concerts, plus a splendid villa quarter will come as something of a surprise to visitors to Cienfuegos (pop. 123,000). It should not be overlooked. The town feels almost duty-bound to live up to its old reputation as the 'Pearl of the South'. Cienfuegos experienced its heyday during the last century, when the harbour was used for the export of sugar, tobacco and tropical fruit. The authorities have recently been trying to re-create its former grandeur. Something of the town's earlier Bohemian atmosphere has been restored in the former villa peninsula of Punta Gorda. Some time ago, plans to complete the construction of a nuclear power station, stopped in the wake of the Chernobyl disaster, have now been officially put on the shelf.

Parque Martí

☺ Spacious, grassy square with a round music pavilion and rows of seating, surrounded entirely by restored buildings, such as the Teatro Tomás Terry (1895) and the Palacio de Cultura. Generally agreed to be one of Cuba's finest urban open spaces.

Museo Histórico Provincial

Documents, paintings, old furniture and everyday objects, relating to the history of the town and surrounding region.

Parque Martí; admission $2

Cueva del Camarón

The speciality of this seafood restaurant in the Punta Gorda quarter is the innovative combination of chicken and lobster.

Daily 12.00-23.00; Calle 37, no. 2, between Calle 0 and Calle 2a; Category 2; Tel: 0432/82 38

Palacio de Valle

★ Gothic, Napoleonic neoclassical and, above all, Moorish features are combined in this villa. The wealthy Spaniard, Cicle de Valle y Blanco, had it built in 1913 for $2 million. The rooms on the ground floor are occupied by the restaurant. House specialities are seafood and caviar.

Daily 10.00-23.00; Ave. 37, Punta Gorda; Category 1-2; Tel: 0432/ 63 02

HOTELS

Gran Caribe Jagua

Traditional hotel in the villa quarter on the Punta Gorda peninsula. Swimming pool, bar, restaurant, shop. Cuban wedding receptions often held here. 144 rooms.
Calle 37, no. 1, Punta Gorda; Category 2; Tel: 0432/63 66 and 61 90, Fax: 05/33 50 56

Horizontes Rancho Luna

Pleasant hotel, set among newly planted palm trees. Two restaurants, five bars and a swimming pool, plus excursions and diving lessons. 225 rooms.
Carretera de Rancho Luna; Category 2; Tel: 0432/481 20, Fax: 07/33 50 57

Pasacaballo

Concrete building on the edge of the bay. Pool, bar, restaurant and disco in the cellar. 144 rooms.
Carretera de Rancho Luna; 22 km (14 miles); Category 3; Tel: 0432/ 62 12

SPORTS & LEISURE

Diving

Diving enthusiasts will find several excellent places to explore off the Playa Rancho Luna, including underwater caves and a shipwreck. Diving lessons (with certificate) are available from the *Horizontes Rancho Luna* hotel.

SURROUNDING AREA

Castillo de Jagua   (106/C5)

This fortress, which was built in 1740, lies at the narrow entrance

to the bay of Cienfuegos in *Perche*, where many descendants of earlier immigrants from the Balearic Islands live.

Jardín Botánico   (106/C5)

The finest botanical garden in Cuba features 60 different palms, 20 bamboo varieties and a total of 2000 local and foreign plants.
Daily 08.00-16.00; between San Antón and Pepito Tey; admission: $2

JARDINES DEL REY

(108-109/C-D 1-2) This is the name the Cubans have given to their newest paradise resort on the long Archipiélago de Camagüey off the central north coast, Morón and Ciego de Ávila. It consists primarily of the islands of Cayo Coco and Cayo Guillermo which are linked together by bridges and connected to the mainland by the Piedraplén causeway (17 km or just over 10 miles long). Mangrove forests and lagoons dominate the landscape.

On ★ Cayo Coco **(108/C2)** the Cuban government has tried to maintain a balance by creating a region dedicated to tourism, while safeguarding the habitats of the native flora and fauna (159 different species of bird, including a flamingo colony, and some rare aquatic plants). The *Centro de Investigaciones de Ecosistemas Costeros* (Research Centre for Coastal Ecosystems) is responsible for analyzing problems and finding solutions. They have come to the conclusion that the Piedraplén causeway should be undertunnelled to maintain a normal flow of water. This will also enable the *larvifagos*, a fish that feeds on mosquito larvae, to establish itself.

Centro de Investigaciones de Ecosistemas Costeros

Cayo Coco is named after a white heron, known as the *coco blanco*, just one of the unusual species of bird that can be seen here. If you are interested in joining a bird-watching expedition, contact *Félix Flores. Tel: 033/30 11 61 and 30 11 51.*

Cueva del Jabalí

This large coral stone cave about 6 km (4 mi) from the Tryp Cayo Coco hotel is named after the wild boar (Span.: *jabalí*), which is quite common locally. The cave now houses a restaurant with disco. *Daily 09.00-24.00 (with live music and snacks)*

The sales exhibition of the Cuban Cultural Fund in the Cayo Guillermo Villa Cojímar is definitely worth a visit.

Cayo Guillermo Villa Cojímar

Spacious, well-maintained bungalow complex. 212 rooms. *Cayo Guillermo; Category 2-3; Tel: 033/30 17 12, Fax: 33 55 54*

Tryp Cayo Coco

Exclusive holiday hotel complex with its own square and 'town hall', five restaurants, bars and a disco. 458 rooms. *Cayo Coco; Category 1; Tel: 033/30 13 11, Fax: 30 13 86*

The Tryp Cayo Coco holiday complex is a village in its own right

Villa Vigía

Holiday village opened in 1996, set in a tropical garden by Cayo Guillermo beach. 264 rooms.
Cayo Guillermo; Category 2; Tel: 033/233 35, Fax: 30 01 27

Riding

Horseback-riding excursions are arranged by an agency in *Cayo Guillermo Villa Cojímar.*

Water sports

A well-equipped diving centre, surfing (for beginners), catamarans and canoe hire on the beach in front of the hotels.

Morón   (108/C3)

A large sculpture of a rooster in the town centre recalls the old tradition of cockfighting, which originated around Morón. A mechanism inside lets the rooster crow at regular intervals.

PLAYA SANTA LUCÍA

(112/C3) Playa Santa Lucía is a vast white coral sand beach over 20 km (13 mi) long. It is lined with coconut palms, colourful piers, and restaurants. Opposite the western end lies the Cayo Sabinal peninsula, which marks the start of the Archipiélago de Camagüey, and out to sea is a 30 km (19 mi) long coral reef which attracts many divers. Modern hotels have been built by the beach, but there is no town centre, only the attractive fishing village of La Boca in the north. Countless flamingos are visible from the road. Unfortunately, mosquitoes are also abundant, so remember to bring plenty of strong repellent.

Bonsai

Restaurant at the southern end of the hotel zone. Specializes in east Asian dishes, but you will also find good local dishes on the menu.
Daily 10.00-22.00; Zona Residencial; Category 2; Tel: 032/361 01

Artesanía Denia Matías León

This artist, who is a member of the Federation of Cuban Artisans (ACAA), sells her tasteful paper mâché and coral pieces in the *Hotel Tararaco* at the north-western end of the beach. Ask for Denia Matías León.

Club Amigo Mayanabo

Red roof tiles brighten up the concrete, single-storey accommodation quarters. In pleasant gardens by the beach. Large pool, beach bar and cabaret. 225 rooms.
Carretera Nuevitas; Category 2; Tel: 032/361 84, Fax: 36 51 76

Cuatro Vientos

A magnificent pool, a thatched restaurant and pleasant rooms – a perfect setting for holidaymakers. 412 rooms.
Playa Santa Lucía, Nuevitas, Camagüey; Category 2; Tel: 032/36 51 20, Fax: 36 51 42

Golden Tulip Coral

Well-maintained villa complex in a flourishing tropical garden. Swimming pool, bar and restaurant. The hotel is managed by the

Dutch Golden Tulip chain. 278 rooms.

Carretera Nuevitas; Category 2; Tel: 032/36 51 59, Fax: 36 51 53

SPORTS & LEISURE

Diving

The largest diving centre is the *Centro Internacional de Buceo de Marlin* at the northern end of Playa Santa Lucía. There are about 35 attractive diving sites in the vicinity, and excursions are available to all of them. An introductory course for beginners costs $95, a week-long course is $360 (PADI and CMAS).

Riding

The *Golden Tulip Club Caracol* hotel organizes riding excursions.

SURROUNDING AREA

Cayo Sabinal   **(112/B3)**

The hotel agencies arrange boat trips to the *Playa Los Pinos, Playa Brava* (restaurant) and *Playa Bonita*. Sights include a ruined fortress and the *Faro Colón* lighthouse.

La Boca   **(112/C3)**

The highlight of Santa Lucía, only 6 km (4 mi) north of the town centre. Wonderful beach with small, colourful Caribbean stalls. Unfortunately, most of the local fishermen have had to move, as tourism has taken over. Try the fresh lobster at the *Casa del Pescador* or the *Boucanero (open daily from morning until the last customer has gone; Category 2; no telephone).*

TRINIDAD

(107/D6) Founded in 1513 by Velázquez, the city of Trinidad (pop.

36,000) is undoubtedly one of Cuba's touristic highlights. Streets of cobblestone (imported from Boston as ship's ballast), high wooden doors and latticed windows beneath red roofing-tiles, Baroque church towers, and horse-drawn carts for the tourists all contribute to creating a unique atmosphere. As in the case of so many other Cuban cities, Trinidad's wealth was generated in the early 19th century by the sugar boom. The emancipation of the slaves and the War of Independence brought the burgeoning prosperity to a halt, and Trinidad's harbour no longer had a part to play in Cuba's external trade. One outcome of Trinidad's commercial decline is that the heart of the old town has remained almost unchanged. It was declared a national monument in 1950, and in 1989 the UNESCO granted the town, and its Valle de los Ingenios, World Heritage status. Museums, galleries, souvenir shops and restaurants have sprung up to meet the needs of the huge influx of tourists. About 10 minutes away by car lies the broad, white Playa Ancón, so you can combine a journey back into Cuba's colonial history with the pleasures of the beach.

SIGHTS

The Old Town

Trinidad was built on a hill and all the historic streets wind their way around the main square, which is located at the summit. If you stroll up Calle Simón Bolívar, Calle Guinart and Calle Colón, you will get your bearings by the Iglesia la Santísima bell tower.

MUSEUMS

Museum admission prices range from $1 to $2.

Museo de Arqueología Guamuhaya

Artefacts dating from pre-Columbian times shed light on the lives of the Siboney Indians. The skeleton of a slave who died over 130 years ago is used to illustrate how the black workers were mistreated. The body was taken from Trinidad's slave cemetery.
Sat-Thur 08.00-17.00; Simón Bolívar 457

Museo de la Arquitectura

Architectural museum in the former Sánchez-Iznaga residence. Exhibits include models of typical colonial-style buildings as well as door mountings and ornamental gratings.
Tues-Sat 09.00-12.00 and 14.00-18.00, Sun 09.00-13.00; Desengaño 83

Museo de la Lucha Contra Bandidos

The Museum of the Struggle against Counter-revolutionaries documents how, during the 1960s, Cuba's revolutionary army defended the people from political opponents. Exhibits include a boat that exiled Cubans used to cross from Florida and an American spy plane shot down over Cuba.
Tues-Sun 08.00-17.00; Cristo, esq. Boca

Museo Municipal

A local history museum in the former residence of the sugar baron Cantero. One interesting

The palm-ringed Plaza Mayor in the centre of Trinidad

The first Cubans

Pottery fragments, names and legends are about all that has survived from Cuba's aboriginal population. Within the space of a few decades, the 300,000 or so Cuban Indians were almost entirely wiped out. The main causes for their demise were the diseases brought to the island by European settlers. As in many other Caribbean islands, the immune system of the native population had no antibodies against the new strains of bacteria. Forced labour, murder and suicide also contributed to their deaths. One important Indian legacy was the name for the island. Cubanacán was the territory in the centre of the island ruled by a *cazique* (Indian chief) and the state-run tourist organization has adopted its name. Hanabana, Camagüey and Baracoa were also *cazique* kingdoms, whose names have lived on. The famous *cazique*, Hatuey, is remembered in a brand of Cuban beer. He probably came from Hispaniola in order to warn his fellow Indians about the Spanish threat, but he was soon caught and condemned to death as a ringleader. Legend has it that when Hatuey, the first Cuban rebel, was awaiting death at the stake, he refused to be christened, declaring that he did not wish to meet any Spaniards in heaven.

feature is the large old kitchen, which opens out on to the patio. The view from the tower extends over Trinidad's tiled roofs.

Thur-Tues 08.00-17.00; Simón Bolívar 423

Museo Romántico

★ Porcelain, crystal chandeliers, glasses, furniture from France and Asia – no museum in Havana has such fine furnishings. Former residents of this house by the Plaza Mayor, which dates from 1740, include the family of Count Nicolás Brunet y Muñoz.

Tues-Sun 08.00-17.00; Fernando Hernández Echemendía 52

RESTAURANTS

El Jigüe

Restaurant in a house dating from 1718. Meat and fish dishes are served with coleslaw, black beans and rice.

Rubén Martínez Villena 69; Category 2-3; Tel: 0419/41 36

La Canchanchara

Meeting place for aficionados of the Canchanchara cocktail, a delicious combination of honey, rum and lemon juice which used to be served in traditional clay mugs, now replaced with plastic cups.

Daily 10.00-22.00; Rubén Martínez Villena

Méson del Regidor

Simple grilled dishes in an old colonial house opposite the municipal museum.

Daily 10.00-18.00; Simón Bolívar 424; Category 2; Tel: 0419/37 56

SHOPPING

Galería de Arte

This gallery exhibits and sells paintings by Cuban artists developing Afro-Cuban themes.

Daily 09.00-17.00; Simón Bolívar 43, esq. Rubén Martínez Villena

Tienda de Arte

Handicrafts, plus drawings and watercolours based on Trinidad. *Simón Bolívar 418*

Ancón

A modern annexe brightens up the renovated main block. Adjacent to the vast white Playa Ancón. Shop, photo developing service and wide selection of excursions. 279 rooms.
Playa Ancón; Category 2; Tel: 0419/ 40 11 and 31 55, Fax: 05/61 20 and 61 21

Motel Horizontes las Cuevas

A basic hotel with swimming pool and children's pool. Only a 10-minute walk to the town centre, and a bus service takes guests to the Playa Ancón. 112 rooms in single-storey double villas.
Finca Santa Ana; Category 3; Tel: 0419/36 24

SURROUNDING AREA

Hanabanilla Reservoir/ Santa Clara   (107/D4-5)

★ The Hanabanilla Reservoir lies in an austere plain of pine trees, about a 30-minute drive from Trinidad in the direction of Santa Clara. It is a popular destination for anglers.

Santa Clara, the capital of Santa Clara province (pop. 172,000), can be reached from Trinidad within an hour. This town was the first stronghold to be captured by the revolutionary forces. Situated on the border between the plain, the Escambray mountains, sugar cane, tobacco and pasture land, it is an important commercial centre. As well as the Teatro Caridad (1885) and the Iglesia del Buen Viaje with its fine wooden ceiling, a visit to the town should also include some of the museums, first and foremost the *Museo de Artes Decorativas (Mon and Wed-Sat 13.00-18.00, Sun 09.00-13.00; Marta Abreu, esq. Luis Estévez)*, which houses a superb collection of valuable European furniture and furnishings from the 18th and 19th centuries. The *Museo Che Guevara* documents Che Guevara's military strategy of 1958 *(Tues-Sat 13.00-18.00, Sun 09.00-13.00; Ciudad Escolar Abel Santamaría, Reparto Osvaldo Herrera)*.

Hotel recommendation: The *Hotel Horizontes Caneyes* is situated in a palm-shaded garden with swimming pool. 91 rooms. *Ave. de los Eucalyptos y Circunvalación de Santa Clara; Category 2; Tel: 0422/ 45 12, Fax: 07/33 50 09*

Zaza Reservoir/ Sancti Spíritus   (108/A4)

As you head out of Trinidad in a north-easterly direction towards Sancti Spíritus, you will soon pass the small Zaza Reservoir, a picturesque spot surrounded by clumps of royal palms. Sancti Spíritus (pop. 72,000) is only an hour's drive from here. The town is famed for its *puntos espirituales*, high-spirited singing duels which are typical of the region. The *Escambray* theatre group also enjoys a country-wide reputation.

Hotel recommendation: *Horizontes Zaza* is a decent hotel close to the Zaza Reservoir. 128 rooms. *Finca San José, Lago Zaza; Category 3; Tel: 0412/60 12 and 53 34*

Afro-Cuban culture and dream beaches

From lively Santiago de Cuba to Baracoa, Cuba's oldest town, and on to the holiday paradise of Guardalavaca

The Cubans who live in the eastern part of the island seem less inhibited and more cheerful than their compatriots in Havana, the crowded capital of 2.1 million inhabitants (about one fifth of the island's total population). A vast majority of eastern Cubans are descended from African slaves who first arrived on slave ships via Santiago de Cuba, many of whom then followed French settlers inland. In many respects, the eastern half of Cuba has always been ahead of the rest of the island. In pre-Columbian times, large settlements in the area were ruled by *caziques*, or Indian chiefs. Excavations at the burial sites in the Holguín region brought to light some fascinating finds, among the most interesting in the whole of the Caribbean region. In the far east, Cuba's first Spanish governor, Diego Velázquez, founded Baracoa, the island's first town. After Santo Domingo in the Dominican Republic, Baracoa is, in fact, the oldest town in the whole of the Americas. In Santiago de Cuba, Velázquez used what is said to be the oldest house on the island as both his office and private residence; it is now a museum.

It was also in these parts that the seeds of the Revolution germinated – and with considerable bloodshed, as the museums of Santiago de Cuba testify. The Playa de los Colorados, just south of Bayamo, was the spot where, in December 1956, after a stormy crossing from Mexico, the *Granma* landed with its cargo of rebels. The few survivors from the first unsuccessful coup later took refuge in the island's highest mountains, the Sierra Maestra.

Behind the beautiful beaches which line the north-facing coast of the channel between Cuba and the Bahamas is a hilly hinterland, which becomes mountainous as you head further inland. Thanks to some new hotel development towns such as Guardalavaca, with its long coral sand beach cooled by deciduous forest, have become popular tourist resorts. Its counterpart in the south, by the coast near Santiago de Cuba, is the huge

The cathedral in Santiago de Cuba, the southernmost town on Cuba

MARCO POLO SELECTION: THE EAST

1 Casa de Velázquez in Santiago de Cuba
The oldest house in Cuba, once the residence of Cuba's first Spanish governor and now a colonial museum (page 79)

2 Museo Chorro de Maita in Banes
Unique museum beside an Indian burial site (page 76)

3 Transport Museum in the Parque Nacional de Bacanao
A 1914 Thunderbird, an old Austin, a Buick and a 1920s Ford — just four from this wonderful collection of vintage cars (page 85)

4 Casa de Trova in Santiago de Cuba
Jazz and atmosphere in Cuba's most unusual bar (page 82)

Bacanao leisure park, now under UNESCO protection. The main attractions here include beaches in tiny, romantic bays framed by rocks, a museum of vintage cars, and a dinosaur park.

GUARDALAVACA

(116/A1) Together with Santiago de Cuba on the Caribbean coast, Guardalavaca, with its *Don Lino* and *Esmeralda* beaches, is the main tourist centre in the east of the island. It is the ideal place to combine seaside relaxation with cultural excursions — a trip to the beautiful Mayabe valley, for example, or to the little town of Banes, where an archaeological museum provides an insight into the island's lost Indian culture. The Museum of Natural History in Holguín contains a fine collection of *polymitas*, the brightly-banded snails indigenous to eastern Cuba.

RESTAURANTS

Conuco Mongo Viña
A popular spot with terrace by the bay and a fine view of the lagoon. Pork dishes are a special-

ity. *Jutía congas*, a type of large native rodent, are kept in the garden.
Daily 08.00-20.00 (extended hours when busy); Guardalavaca; Category 2-3; Tel: 024/302 48

El Cayuelo
Situated by the wilder, eastern section of Playa Guardalavaca. Sit down for a meal of freshly-caught fish or lobster and enjoy the sea view while dining. Simple rooms are available upstairs for $15 per person per night.
Daily 09.00-21.00 (extended hours when busy); Playa Guardalavaca; Category 3; no telephone

Pizza Nova
Popular meeting place in the hotel zone. Serves pasta dishes as well as pizzas.
Daily 09.00-23.00 (or longer); Playa Guardalavaca; Category 3; Tel: 024/ 301 37

SHOPPING

The shops in Playa Guardalavaca's Centro Comercial sell mainly sportswear, perfumes and souvenirs. There is also a supermarket.

Atlántico

Not so new, but still a popular beach hotel; babysitting service, playrooms and swimming pool and children's paddling pool. 232 rooms.

Playa Guardalavaca, Banes; Category 2; Tel: 024/301 80, Fax: 33 50 73

Delta Las Brisas

A new beach hotel under Canadian management, with a distinctive north American atmosphere. Spacious layout, and full leisure facilities including aerobics, riding and windsurfing. 230 rooms.

Playa Guardalavaca; Category 2; Tel: 024/302 18

Sol Río de Mares

Hotel belonging to the Spanish chain, Sol and Meliá, by the Esmeralda beach, 1 km from Playa Guardalavaca. The nearby *Río de Luna* is under the same management. Stylish, but relaxed and informal atmosphere. The multi-storey block surrounds a large pool area. 242 rooms (including 2 for disabled guests).

Playa Esmeralda, Carretera Guardalavaca; Category 1-2; Tel: 024/300 30, Fax: 300 35

Villa Don Lino

A no-frills holiday hotel with simple rooms, but a good events programme. The variety show on the *Santa María*, a replica of Columbus' ship, draws audiences from other hotels. 145 rooms.

Playa Blanca; Category 3; Tel: 024/204 43

Villa Turey

Sprawling two-storey hotel village near the beach. Large lagoon-style swimming pool, surrounded by restaurants and bar. 136 rooms.

Playa Guardalavaca; Category 2-3; Tel: 024/301 95, Fax: 302 65

Diving

Jan and Marian Snijders run a diving centre at the *Sol Río de Mares* hotel. They offer courses for both beginners and experienced divers.

Fax: 024/33 55 71

La Roca

☉ A spacious disco which opens out onto the sea-view terrace. Popular with locals and tourists.

Daily from 21.30; admission $3; Tel: 024/31 67

Banes   (116/A1-2)

This town, which lies some 34 km (22 mi) from Guardalavaca, is famous for its archaeological museums. The *Museo Indocubano Baní* (*Tues-Sat 12.00-18.00, Sun 14.00-18.00; General Marrero 305*) is named after a once-powerful *cazique*, who the conquistadores encountered in the Holguín region. The museum houses 1000 exhibits found in the graves of Indians, most of whom belonged to the Maniabón Taino tribe. These finds represent only a fraction of the 14 million pieces that were found at the various burial sites. Among the artefacts were a number of tiny clay figures. These were probably votive offerings which were buried with the deceased to provide protection on his or her journey into the afterlife. One golden statuette in particular shows obvious central American influences.

The ★ *Museo Chorro de Maita* (*Tues-Sat 09.00-17.00, Sun 09.00-13.00; Chorro de Maita*), 28 km or 17 miles away, displays 62 of the Indian skeletons, between 108 and 2000 years old, which were unearthed at the end of the 1980s in Chorro de Maita, just east of Banes. This place is thought to be the largest Indian burial site in the Caribbean. The bones have been laid out in the museum on plaster boards, in the exact position in which they were found, many with arms crossed across their chests.

Cayo Bariay   (115/F1)

Sixteen statues of Indian gods, surrounded by Greek columns in the shape of a ship's hull, recall 29 October 1492, when Christopher Columbus first set foot on Cuban soil. The memorial by the Gibara road, completed in 1992, is by artist Caridad Ramos Mosquera.

Cayo Naranjo   (115/F1)

This island offshore to the west has its own marine aquarium with dolphins. Organized excursions usually include a visit to the restaurant.

Cayo Saetía   (116/A2)

This fertile island is a habitat for zebra and local breeds of deer. Excursions by helicopter or bus, with restaurant visit included, are organized by the hotels.

Holguín   (115/E2)

The commercial centre for sugar cane, tobacco and livestock in the north-east of the island, and the capital of Cuba's fourth-largest province (pop. 195,000), Holguín lies about 80 km (50 mi) inland and is a good hour's drive from Guardalavaca. It was named after the Spanish sea captain Francisco García Holguín who founded the town in 1523.

Holguín boasts many parks, gardens, interesting town centre sights, such as the *Cathedral San Isidoro* (1720), various functional buildings and factories (textiles, furniture, leather). It is situated between the Mayabe valley and the Loma de la Cruz hill. If you're feeling energetic you can climb the flight of 450 steps to the top.

The *Museo de Ciencias Carlos de la Torre* (*Sun-Thur 09.00-17.00, Sat 13.00-17.00; Maceo/Plaza Central*), in an old building called La Periquera, has a large collection of snail and mussel shells, while the *Museo Provincial* (*Mon-Fri 09.00-17.00, Sat 09.00-13.00; Frexes 198*) contains the prized Holguín Ax, a 30 cm (12 in) high pre-Columbian figure of an elongated man made of polished rock. Other exhibits illustrate the role played by the town during the War of Independence. Souvenir hunters may be interested in the doll factory (*Mon-Sat 08.00-16.30; Fábrica de Muñeca folklórica, Carretera Gibar 560*) and the tobacco factory.

Rafael, the Havanatur representative, offers invaluable assistance to independent tourists.

The ⌁ *Mirador de Mayabe*, overlooking the Mayabe valley, offers excellent accommodation, with rooms in villas, a pool and a restaurant (*Alturas de Mayabe; 8 km or 5 mi; Category 3; Tel: 024/42 21 60*). Part of the complex is given over to the *Mayabe Finca Museum.*

SANTIAGO DE CUBA

(116/A5) This, the southernmost town in Cuba (pop. 350,000), is characterized by the charm and exuberance of its inhabitants. For about 20 years, up until 1549, the whole of Cuba was ruled from here by Diego Velázquez (also worth a visit is the first town Velázquez founded, Baracoa at the eastern tip of the north coast).

It was in the Caribbean-facing port of Santiago de Cuba, however, that the first slave ships anchored. Given its proximity to Jamaica, which the Spanish lost to the English crown, Santiago soon found itself a target for pirates – mainly English. To defend the town against such raiders, the Castillo del Morro (now fully restored) was built. The French, now allied with Spain against England, sent reinforcements, principally settlers from Haiti. As a result, Santiago became almost completely French in character.

The Castillo del Morro in Santiago de Cuba houses a pirates' museum

Traces of the town's links with France are still in evidence, particularly in names, and even in the music. If you go to the Casa de Trova music bar, you could easily imagine yourself in downtown New Orleans, a comparison that would make the ageing Cuban musicians smile wryly. In Santiago de Cuba, you will rarely hear a pro-American word. Most of the inhabitants of Santiago de Cuba are proud to be at the heart of the Cuban Revolution, which explains why the near-by US military base at Guantánamo is regarded by Cubans as a thorn in the flesh.

Several museums document the events which changed the course of history in Santiago de Cuba: the attack on the Moncada barracks, the death of the 22-year-old resistance fighter Frank País, the speech that Castro made in his defence at his trial, the withdrawal of the rebels into the Sierra Maestra, and the announcement of victory from the balcony of the town hall.

Today the atmosphere of the town is very different. The parks and squares bustle with activity, and increasing numbers of tourists congregate in them to enjoy the lively atmosphere and exuberance of the locals.

There are a number of good hotels along the coast, while the Parque Baconao on the outskirts of the town has many attractions, including a dinosaur park, a car museum and wilderness trails.

SIGHTS

Calle Padre Pico

This long staircase flanked by small houses links the lower town with the upper town. It is now a much-photographed spot.

Castillo del Morro/ Museo del Piratería

◁▷ This well-preserved fortress at the entrance to the bay affords a fine view over the sea. The pirate museum documents the history of Caribbean piracy from the 16th century to the 'Yankee' imperialism of the 1900s. Exhibits include lead bullets and chains used for restraining prisoners.
Tues-Sun 09.00-18.00

Cayo Granma

This island in the bay of Santiago de Cuba is home to about 1500 people, and noted for its attractive, Caribbean-style wooden huts, some built above the water on stilts. One hut has been turned into a popular tourist restaurant called *Villa Lurdita*. Boat trips depart from Punta Gorda.

Cementerio Santa Ifigenia

At the heart of this fascinating cemetery lies the grave of the poet and national hero, José Martí. Other well-known figures buried here include the Bacardí family and Carlos Manuel de Céspedes, another much-revered patriot. At one time the dead were segregated by class, and there is a huge contrast between the massive mausoleums on one side and the ordinary unadorned graves on the other.
Ave. Crombet

Parque Céspedes

Parque Céspedes is a focal point for both tourists and locals. Look out for the black-stained wooden balcony on the wall of Casa de Velázquez (1522). Now a colonial museum, this building is reckoned to be the oldest house on Cuba. To the south-west stands the cathedral, and next to that are the *Casa Grande* and the Ayuntamiento or town hall from whose blue balcony Fidel Castro proclaimed the victory of the Cuban revolution on 1 January 1959.

MUSEUMS

Museum admission prices range from $1 to $2.

Casa Natal Antonio Maceo

A typical middle-class home dating from around 1830, where freedom fighter Antonio Maceo grew up. The museum documents his life.

Mon-Sat 08.00-18.30; Los Maceos 207, between Corona and Rastro

Granjita Siboney

About 100 of Fidel Castro's fighters met here to plan the attack on the Moncada barracks. They hid their weapons in the garden fountain.

Tues-Sun 09.00-17.00; Carretera Siboney; 13.5 km/8½ mi)

Museo de Ambiente Histórico Cubano/Casa de Velázquez

★ Built in 1522 by Cuba's first Spanish governor, Diego Velázquez, the museum in the Casa de Velázquez offers fascinating insights into early colonial architecture, and the interior furnishings that were fashionable in the 18th and 19th centuries. One interesting exhibit is the *tinajero*, a porous stone on a stand, which was used for filtering water.

Mon-Sat 08.00-18.00; Sun 09.00-13.00; Parque Céspedes

Museo de Carnaval

Masks, costumes, traditional musical instruments, such as congas and French drums (*tambor francés*), posters and photos evoke the colourful atmosphere of the 10-day carnival, which starts on 25 July in Santiago de Cuba.

Tues-Fri 09.00-17.00; Heredia 330

Museo de la Clandestinidad

The Museum of the Underground Struggle is housed in a former colonial mansion. Once the police headquarters under Batista, the building was fire-bombed in 1956 by Castro's guerrillas. The museum is dedicated to the 22-year-old underground leader Frank País, who was shot dead in 1957.

Tues-Sat 09.00-13.00, Sun 09.00-12.00; Padre Pico

Museo Histórico 16 de Julio/ Cuartel Moncada

Named after a general in the Wars of Independence, these barracks housed the second-largest contingent of Fulgencio Batista's troops before the Revolution. Bullet holes in the walls have been left as reminders of the revolutionaries' brave assault on the stronghold on 16 July 1953. The strategy for attack had been planned earlier by Fidel Castro in the Granjita Siboney. Displays in the museum give a full account of the failed offensive.

Mon-Sat 08.00-18.00, Sun 08.00-12.00

Museo La Isabelica

↘↙ The former *finca* that once belonged to French coffee planter Victor Constantin is now a museum which displays the tools and machinery used in the processing of coffee. The villa lies to the east of town in the Sierra Gran Piedra National Park. For a view of the surrounding country, climb the Big Rock ('La Gran Piedra'). *Tues-Sat 09.00-17.00, Sun 09.00-13.00; Carretera Gran Piedra; 14 km/9 mi*

Museo Provincial Emilio Bacardí

Archaeology and colonial art, records and documents relating to the history of Santiago de Cuba. *Tues-Sat 09.00-18.00, Sun 09.00-13.00; Pío Rosada, esq. Aguilera*

RESTAURANTS

Boca Jagua

Popular restaurant with day trippers. By the beach of the same name in the Parque Nacional de Baconao. Menu recommendations include grilled mackerel, washed down with lemonade made from fresh lemons. *Daily 08.00-21.00; Parque Nacional de Baconao; Category 3*

Casa de Té

❋ Tea house by the Parque Céspedes, where you can sit among the locals and sample a variety of teas from peppermint tea at 20 centavos to jasmine tea from China for 40 centavos. *Mon-Sat 09.00-19.00; Aguilera 30, esq. San Pedro; Category 3*

El Cayo

◁▷ Situated on Granma island in Santiago Bay, this waterside fish restaurant on stilts enjoys a great view of the harbour, the town and the bay. El Cayo has a reputation for serving the best fresh fish in the whole of Santiago. Boats leave from Punta Gorda. *Daily 12.00-18.00; Category 3*

El Morro

◁▷ Enjoy the sea view while you eat, then adjourn to the bar ❋ for a chat with the locals. Specialities include creole dishes, eg *rollito de tasajo*, fish-filled pancakes. *Daily 09.00-21.00; Castillo del Morro; Category 2-3; Tel: 0226/915 76*

Pavo Real

High-ceilinged rooms, long tables, stained-glass windows and festive lights enhance the gastronomic experience provided by the imaginative cuisine. The restaurant is part of the Tropicana theatre complex. *Tues-Sun 12.00-23.00; Autopista Nacional; 1.5 km/1 mi; Category 1-2; Tel: 0226/430 36, 428 14 , 410 71*

Salón 1900

Marble, Art Nouveau chandeliers, and porcelain knick-knacks create a splendid atmosphere. By Cuban standards, the quality of the food is well above average. Try the *sopa de mariscos* (fish soup). *Tues-Sun 19.00-02.00; San Basílico, esq. San Félix; Category 1-2; Tel: 0226/35 07*

SHOPPING

Bazaar

The widest choice of souvenirs in Santiago. Afro-Cuban sculptures, unusual clothes, good watercolours by Cuban artists, books, postcards and so on. *Daily 09.00-17/18.00; Calle 8, no. 301, between Calle 11 and Calle 13, Vista Alegre*

Canay/Bacardí Rum Factory

After a tour of the factory, visitors are invited to browse around the shop, where you can pick up a bottle of 15-year-old rum for about \$15, seven-year-old for about \$8 and five-year and three-year-old rum for about \$6.

Ave. Jesús Menéndez, opposite the new station

La Maison

White villa full of ideas for souvenir hunters: clothes, jewellery, T-shirts and music, plus a well-stocked bar. The garden is used as a venue for upmarket fashion shows held in the evening.

Ave. Manduley 52, Vista Alegre; Tel: 0226/432 65

Amigo Bucanero

Well-managed, sports-orientated hotel on a rocky beach promontory, surrounded by rocks and tropical plants. Activities centre around the pool. 200 rooms.

Carretera Baconao; 4 km/2½ mi; Arroyo La Costa; Category 2; Tel: 0226/545 96

Casa Grande

Splendid turn-of-the-century 'grand hotel' lavishly renovated

Strong modern lines: the Santiago de Cuba hotel

by the Cuban Gran Caribe chain. 55 rooms.

Parque Céspedes; Category 2; Tel: 0226/866 00, Fax: 860 35

Horizontes Las Américas

Furnishings are simple, but the hotel has every amenity, from travel agent to swimming pool. 68 rooms.

Ave. Las Américas; Category 3; Tel: 0226/420 11

Los Corales LTI

Quiet holiday hotel, with large pool and gardens spread out over a wide area by the Playa Cazonal. Tennis, riding, car and motor-cycle hire. Entertainment for children. 118 rooms.

Parque Nacional de Baconao; Category 2; Tel: 0226/861 77 or 27 191, Fax: 861 77 or 861 29

Santiago de Cuba

♔ Santiago's top central hotel. Fitness room and swimming pool with jacuzzi are just some of the amenities available in this huge glass, steel and concrete structure. It sometimes seems as if the whole of Santiago meets up in the disco. 290 rooms.

Ave. Las Américas/Calle M; Category 2; Tel: 0226/426 12, Fax: 417 56

Versalles

Modern hotel near the airport. Panoramic restaurants. 46 rooms in bungalows and villas.

Barrio Versalles; Category 3; Tel: 0226/910 14

ENTERTAINMENT

Cabaret San Pedro

Variety show with music and dancing in a room which is reminiscent of an old school hall. Fine view out to sea from the terrace.
Wed-Mon from 21.00

Casa de Trova

★ A New Orleans-style atmosphere, where ageing musicians give a history lesson in Afro-Cuban music. They may be 70 years old, but they can still play the trumpet like Pepe Sánchez. The *trova* is a ballad form which originated in Santiago. It is a synthesis of African percussion and Spanish guitar.

Mon-Sat from 16.00, Sun (the best day) from 09.00; Heredia

Sábado de Rumba

❂ Saturday nights, the Calle Heredia is closed to traffic and many local groups perform in the street. The concerts are free and popular with locals and tourists alike.

Sat 21.00-23.00; Heredia

Tropicana

A less formal version of the famous variety show staged by the sister company in Havana. Visitors from other counties are ceremoniously welcomed. The sound quality is less than perfect, and the show soon turns into an audience participation event.

Daily 10.30-03.00; Autopista Nacional, 1.5 km/1 mi; Tel: 0226/410 71

SURROUNDING AREA

Baracoa   (117/E3-4)

Although the town has an important place in the first chapter of Cuba's colonial history, it does have an end of the world feel about it. Columbus erected a large wooden cross when he landed here on his first journey in 1492. Twenty years later, Velázquez chose the same spot for

Cuba's first town. The island, which at that time was ruled by the *caziques,* retained Baracoa as its capital until 1524. Hatuey, who had escaped from the Spanish on Hispaniola, joined forces with the Cuban *caziques* in Baracoa and tried to organize a rebellion against the European invaders. But it came to nothing; Hatuey was captured and executed.

The few remains of old fortresses (eg the *Hotel Horizontes El Castillo; 35 rooms; Calixto Garcia, Loma del Paraiso; Category 3; Tel: 0214/21 03*) serve as a reminder that in the early days this coastline regularly came under attack from pirates. Baracoa lies on the rivers Duaba, Toa and Miel at the edge of the Sierra Maestra. One of the foothills, the 589 m (1950 ft) high Yunque mountain, dominates the Baracoa horizon and is easily visible to seafarers. Archaeologists have found shells and skeletons at the top of this square peak, and it is thought that Taino Indians assembled here for tribal meetings and ceremonies.

Baracoa's 50,000 inhabitants keep Cuba supplied with coffee, cocoa, bananas and coconuts grown on the plantations in the hilly interior. Historically, the most interesting features of the town are the *Cruz de la Parra* (Columbus' Cross of the Vine), which is now in the cathedral for safe-keeping, the *Fortaleza de la*

Gods and sacred cults

Compared to other Caribbean islands, relatively few descendants of African slaves live on Cuba, but nevertheless the old African myths are still very much alive. Many of the communities in the east of the island still cling to the beliefs of the Santoría cult. It was to this part of the island that many French refugees and their slaves fled after the rebellion against slavery on Hispaniola, when the Republic of Haiti was founded. Like voodoo on Haiti and *candomblé* in Salvador de Bahia in Brazil, during the ritual gatherings of the *santeros,* the priests, pleas are made to the *orishas,* the 20 or so good or evil deities. Followers believe that every person is allocated to one of these deities, eg Ochún the god of vanity, Oyá the dangerous goddess of revenge, Yemayá the goddess of the sea and motherhood, or Ogún, the ladies' man, warrior and god of the mountains. For many black Cubans, it is usual to have two altars in the house: one Christian and one African. In the Spanish era, the African gods were assigned to Christian saints. The gods have continued to be worshipped in this way despite pressure from the church to deny their existence. Since the Revolution of 1959 the cult, which had been suppressed by the religious authorities, has enjoyed greater social acceptance; in the meantime the role of the Catholic church has been downplayed. Cuba has thus become the only country with a black population in the New World, apart from Haiti and Brazil, where ritual ceremonies, often involving animal sacrifices, did not have to be performed in secret. The rituals are enacted in the hotels for tourists, but are usually described as dances.

Punta (1803) by the harbour and the *Fortaleza de Matachín* (1802), which now houses the informative local history museum, the *Museo Municipal de Baracoa (Tues-Sat 09.00-17.00, Sun 09.00-13.00)*. Also look out for the *la Farola viaduct* and the impressive ⇗ *Alto de Cotilla* panorama.

Bayamo (115/D4)

The picturesque area around this friendly town is dotted with rice fields spread out along the banks of the Río Cauto, at 350 km or 220 miles the longest of Cuba's rivers. Don't forget your camera on this trip – the backdrop of the Sierra Maestra mountains will provide the inspiration for some memorable photographs.

Bayamo (pop. 105,000) is the capital of the Granma Province. It is named after the sailing boat in which the revolutionaries landed at Playa de los Colorados in 1956. Several museums in the town concentrate on the political his-

The coastline near Guantánamo: 'a thorn in the flesh' of the Cuban government

tory of the region, which is regarded as the cradle of the liberation movement. The Estrella Tropical freemason's lodge, which played an important role in the War of Independence, was founded here in 1868.

It was also in Bayamo that the legendary landowner Carlos Manuel de Céspedes freed his slaves and then led them into battle against the Spanish. Other landowners soon followed his example. The *Museo Casa Natal Carlos Manuel de Céspedes* (*Tues-Sat 12.00-19.00, Sun 09.00-13.00; Maceo 47*) documents the life of this Cuban hero.

Next door, the *Museo Provincial* (*Tues-Sat 08.00-18.00, Sun 09.00-13.00*) houses some archaeological finds, and it also tells the story of the town fire of 1868. The proud townsfolk started the fire themselves as they did not want their homes to fall into the hands of the Spanish.

Not far from the Museo Provincial stands the 200-year-old parish church, noted for its magnificent Baroque altars. The church has now been declared a national monument.

El Cobre (115/F5)

This place of pilgrimage, which is also the centre of the copper mining industry, lies about 20 minutes by car from Santiago de Cuba, in the mountains beyond Melgarejo. The basilica which crowns the hilltop was built in 1927 and is visible for miles. Guarding the altar inside the church is the patron saint of Cuba, the *Virgen de la Claridad*. The copper mine slag heaps in the valley can be seen from the car park.

Guantánamo (116/C4)

This town (pop. 150,000) has been immortalized by the song *Guantanamera* ('girl from Guantánamo'). It is a good hour's drive from Santiago de Cuba and, although it has an even more Caribbean feel than Santiago, Guantánamo has little to offer the tourist. When sugar exports were at their highest, almost 50% of the population were slave workers. Most people bypass the town on their way to the Bahía de Guantánamo, a US naval base that has been here since 1903, Castro referred to it as a 'dagger plunged into the heart of Cuban soil'. Under the treaty, 115 sq km (45 sq mi) of strategically important natural harbour were leased to the United States for 99 years. The bay and installations can be seen from an outlying wall.

Parque Nacional de Baconao (116/B5)

Since the release of Steven Spielberg's *Jurassic Park*, the prehistoric valley in the Baconao National Park, 22 km (14 mi) south of Santiago de Cuba, has become a major attraction in eastern Cuba. Some 250 life-sized model dinosaurs look on benignly as the tourists parade in front of them, cameras clicking. There is also a small museum. The Valle de la Prehistoria actually only covers a small part of this 80,000-hectare (200,000 acre) national park. Adults will be drawn to the ★ *Museo Nacional del Transporte* (*daily 09.00-17.00*) where 34 vintage American cars, mostly from the 1920s (the oldest was made in 1912), and over 2000 models are displayed in three exhibition halls.

Touring the Island Highlights

These routes are marked in green on the map inside front flap and in the road atlas beginning on page 100

These routes are marked in green on the map inside front flap and in the road atlas beginning on page 100

① THE GREEN WEST: ORCHIDS, CAVES AND FERTILE EARTH

This tour leads through 250 km or 155 miles of what is geologically the oldest and the most fertile part of the island: to nature reserves with tropical vegetation, to thermal springs, to the tobacco town of Pinar del Río and to its fertile hinterland. An overnight stay in the fabulously beautiful Viñales valley is recommended before returning.

You leave *Havana (p. 37)* via the Avenida de Rancho Boyeros and, still within the city limits, take the entrance to the motorway leading in a westerly direction to Pinar del Río. On a slope of the *Sierra del Rosario*, approximately 80 km (50 mi) from the capital, lies the little village of *Soroa (p. 50)*, named after a former landowner, with a nearby orchid garden. At the village restaurant, *Castillo de las Nubes* (creole and international cuisine, *Category 3*), you can fortify yourself for the journey ahead which will take you back to the motorway. About 15 km (10 mi) to the west you will reach the access road to *San Diego*

de los Baños branching off to your right. This small spa resort (modern facilities with thermal springs) nestles into the mountains behind, in which you find La Güira National Park. The next destination, the old tobacco town of *Pinar del Río (p. 49)* is still about 55 km (45 mi) away. One can reach it via the mountain road at the foot of the Cordilleras, or take the quicker route on the motorway.

After visiting Pinar del Río you will come to the loveliest landscape along this route. You leave the town by the same road that you came, but instead of going back onto the motorway you continue straight ahead in a northerly direction towards Viñales. From Pinar del Río the road takes you for about half an hour through a gentle, hilly countryside with small, simple cottages surrounded by gardens in bloom, to the village of *Viñales* (restaurant tip: *Don Tomás*, speciality: paella, *Category 2-3*). As you go, you will see low wooden racks carefully hung with tobacco leaves. The world's best tobacco is dried here. Beyond the village of Viñales, signposts point the way to the *Mural de la Prehistoria*, a tall (120 m/400 ft) cliff face on which the painter Leovigildo

Gonzales depicted the history of evolution in the 1970s. At its foot is a roofed open-air restaurant specializing in one dish: grilled pork with *yame* root, salad and *arroz con frijoles* (rice with black beans).

A breathtaking view over the Viñales valley, now increasingly popular with independent travellers, is one of the attractions of the *Los Jazmines* hotel (*78 rooms; Category 2-3; Tel: 08/33404, Fax: 07/335042*).

Not far away are two natural caves. The *Cueva de Viñales* houses a cabaret featuring a daily programme (*20.00-01.00*) with music, dance and a show. A short drive away is the *Cueva del Indio* (*admission $3*), inhabited by bats and partly navigable by boat.

② ACROSS CENTRAL CUBA: FROM THE NICEST BEACH TO THE NICEST CITY

You should plan at least two days, better yet three or four, for this tour, since there are so many things to see: vast sugar-cane fields, crocodiles, a World Heritage city and some of the most beautiful mountain lakes. The first stretch is about 300 km (185 miles) long and leads via Cienfuegos to the deep south and to the city of Trinidad on the Caribbean coast, with a short side-trip to La Boca (don't forget your mosquito repellent!). The return trip takes you through the Escambray Mountains via Sancti Spíritus and Santa Clara (about 400 km/250 miles).

Leaving *Varadero* (*p. 59*) going east, your first stop is *Cárdenas* (*p. 57*). From here you take the coastal road. After 8 km (5 mi) you will come to a gas station where the street branches to the right in the direction of Jagüey Grande (57 km/35 mi), taking you into the interior of the island, past the towns of *Carlos Rojas* and *Jovellanos*, along sugar-cane plantations and past military training camps with fading propaganda murals. At the *Jagüey Grande* petrol station, you cross the motorway heading south for an excursion to the *Laguna del Tesoro* (*p. 59*) with the tourist village of *La Boca*, and then towards *Guamá* (restaurants, souvenir shops, a replica of an old Indian village) where crocodiles are bred for their edible flesh (samples can be had at the restaurant). In addition, you can take an excursion boat to the marshes of *Ciénaga de Zapata* (*p. 58*) with their rich wildlife. Continue back to the motorway and drive eastward. At Cartagena, turn south towards Congojas (14 km/9 mi), going through *Ariza* and on to *Cienfuegos* (*p. 64*), the 'Pearl of the South.' Calle 37 (*Prado*) will take you directly to the residential quarter of Punta Gorda with its villas and the first-class restaurant in the Palacio del Valle, a castle of dreams. The undisputed highlight of the tour, however, is the old city of *Trinidad* (*p. 68*), rated by UNESCO as World Heritage site, some 79 km or 50 mi from Cienfuegos. The approaching road runs so close to the coast that in April, it is covered with crabs crushed by vehicles. Trinidad, nearly 500 years old, makes a picturesque sight with narrow cobblestone streets meandering up and down the hills. In the restaurant *Mesón del Regidor* (*Bolívar 424, at the corner of*

Colón; Category 2), guests can dine in the living-room of the former inspector royal. The hotels are located outside the city on the marvellously wide *Playa Ancón* (budget-priced, although an ugly concrete structure, is the *Costasur, Category 2-3; Tel: 0419/61 00*). One should begin the return drive early and well-rested, since it is more tiresome than the drive there, not least due to the tortuous road across the *Escambray Mountains.* You are well rewarded, however, by spectacular views out over the Caribbean and the beautiful, dark *Zaza Reservoir* near *Sancti Spíritus* (*p. 71*). In this city, capital of the province of the same name, one should visit the Parroquial Mayor Espíritu Santo, in which Bartolomé de Las Casas, famous advocate for the Indians, is said to have preached. The ceiling of the church is made of fine Cuban wood. Some 20 km/12 mi to the north-west, you arrive back on the motorway winding through the green valleys of the *Alturas de Santa Clara* (*p. 71*).

③ BACK TO THE ROOTS: FROM GUARDALAVACA TO BARACOA

 This route, which is around 500 km (300 miles) long and takes three days to complete, leads you to the sites most associated with the Spanish conquest, the Indians' resistance, the time of slavery and the beginnings of the Revolution. We recommend that you incorporate your stops into both outward and return journeys.

Leaving *Guardalavaca* (*p. 74*), you head west and continue along the coast. After about 24 km/15 mi you reach the *Bariay* peninsula with the Columbus Monument. Continuing past *Aguas Claras*, you will come to *Holguín* (*p. 76*). From the *Mirador de Mayabe* restaurant you can enjoy a magnificent view of the deep valley of the Río Holguín and the Sierra Maestra mountain range beyond. The journey continues onwards for another 71 km (44 mi) in a south-westerly direction to *Bayamo* (*p. 84*) at the foot of the Sierra. To the west of this capital of Granma province lies the plain of Río Cauto extending all the way to the bay of Guacanayabo. It was here that Fidel Castro, Che Guevara and the other revolutionaries landed in 1956, having crossed over from Mexico in a yacht called *Granma*, and went on to hide in the mountains of the *Sierra Maestra.* The journey through this homeland of the revolution will take you through the foothills of the Sierra past *Jiguaní* and the *América* reservoir dam towards Santiago de Cuba. At Palma Soriano, there is an access road leading to the new motorway which takes you directly to *Santiago de Cuba* (*p. 77*). This city also played an important role in the revolution, and is well worth an overnight stay. A visit to the fortress of *El Morro* is certain to take you back to the age of pirates. Before continuing on to Barocoa (200 km/125 mi), a good-night's sleep and an early start are recommended. The road via Moa is in very poor condition, therefore, it is better to leave the town in a north-easterly direction via *El Cristo, Alto Sango* and *La Maya,* and take the motorway to the U.S. naval base of *Guantánamo* (*p. 85*). From here, the road continues along the Caribbean coastline, with the Sierra Maestra mountain range behind you rising out of the new, still rather inaccessible, Alexander von Humboldt National Park. *Cajobabo* marks the beginning of a tortuous mountain road to *Baracoa* (*p. 82*), Cuba's oldest city. The fortress-*cum*-hotel *El Castillo* (*Category 2; Tel: 021/421 47, Fax: 0226/860 74*) provides a welcome respite from the journey with a great view of El Yunque, the mountain from which the Indians communicated with their gods.

④ THE CAYOS AND PLAYAS OF THE NORTH

 This journey, approx. 250 km (155 mi) long, is for those who wish to see some of the neighbouring holiday resorts. If you're staying on Cayo Coco or Cayo Guillermo, take a trip to Playa Santa Lucía – or vice versa.

Let's assume your holiday resort is *Playa Santa Lucía* (*p. 67*). Call the hotel *Villa Cojímar* on *Cayo Guillermo* (*Category 2-3; Tel: 033/30 17 12, Fax: 33 55 54*) to make a reservation for the following night so you will at least have a place to stay when you arrive. To go to Cayo Coco or Cayo Guillermo from Playa Santa Lucía, leave the resort using the only road which leads in a south-westerly direction, and head towards *Camagüey* (*p. 62*). Once past the verdant plains of the Rosalia, Molina, and Najarro rivers, the road slowly begins to ascend at Santa Isabel. After about 80 km (50 mi) you will reach Camagüey, the administrative centre of the province, where two appealing restaurants are found on the Plaza San Juan de Dios, both

of which have outside terraces upon which to dine. Once refreshed, you continue for another hour before you get to *Ciego de Ávila*. Apart from being the centre of the livestock industry, and the landing site for German charter flights, the town has little to offer for the sightseer. Continue towards the Atlantic, and you will soon find yourself in a pleasant landscape with wide-open ranges. After about half an hour you will arrive at *Morón* (*p. 65*), the last major settlement before the Cayos to the north. Many of the island's hotel staff live here. Driving through town along the main street, you will have a view of the Laguna de Leche on your left and the first mangrove bay of the Atlantic coast on your right. Always keeping to the right, you will soon come to the entrance to the Piedraplén, the 17 km (10½ mi) long causeway leading to *Cayo Coco* (*p. 65*). Only tourists are allowed access to the causeway, and stopping at the barrier will give you just enough time to get your camera ready, since you're certain to see swarms of sea birds, and perhaps even flamingos, whilst crossing it. The exit leading to the first notable resort development and to the beautiful *Playa Larga* is still on the causeway, branching off to your left (in a westerly direction). *Cayo Guillermo* to the west and the hotel *Villa Cojímar* can similarly be reached along bridges or causeways.

For the tour in the opposite direction, we recommend that you reserve a room at the reasonably-priced *Club Amigo Mayanabo* (*Category 2; Tel: 032/361 84*) in *Playa Santa Lucía*.

Practical information

Useful addresses and information for your visit to Cuba

BANKS & MONEY

The Cuban currency is the peso (divided into 100 centavos) but tourists are expected to pay for most goods and services in U.S. dollars. The only places you may need to use pesos are at the Mercado Agropecuario in Havana, to pay for the occasional snack or drink bought on the street, and on the service buses which are few and far between. It is not worth buying Cuban currency with dollars at the Banco Nacional de Cuba, as the official exchange rate is 1 to 1. Cubans buy dollars on the black market at a rate of 1 to 26. The government has also introduced a third currency in the form of *B certificados*. These vouchers are often given as change. They have no value outside Cuba, but can be changed back into dollars at the airport. To be on the safe side, you should try to spend them as soon as possible.

The best way to cope with the currency problem is to carry a quantity of cash, especially $1 bills, and a Visa or MasterCard (as long as they have not been issued by an American bank). Both credit cards are widely accepted by car hire companies, excursion organizers, larger hotels and all the main Caracol, or state-run, tourist shops, but less readily by restaurants. American Express and Diners Club cards can be used as payment or for obtaining cash. US travellers' cheques issued by the Bank of America are now accepted by the Asistur agency, and in the bank at the Habana Libre hotel. But travellers' cheques that have been issued by an American bank will not be accepted anywhere.

If you find yourself in financial difficulty because of the unwillingness of businesses to accept credit cards or travellers' cheques, the Asistur agency can arrange for the receipt of money transfers from home; however, you may have to wait three to five days before they pay out. *Asistur's* main office is in Havana: *Paseo del Prado 254, between Calle Trocadero and Calle Ánimas; Tel: 07/62 55 19 and 63 82 84, Fax: 33 80 87*. Branches of Asistur can also be found in Varadero and Santiago de Cuba, but money transfers are always made via Havana.

BUSES

The bus network that once covered both urban Havana and the rest of the country is now in a sorry state. In Havana itself, the number of *guaguas,* as the Cubans call their buses, has been drastically reduced, so travellers are often faced with long queues, especially in the morning rush hour and at the end of the working day. Cubans get around by hitch-hiking, in travel cooperatives or on the Cuban-made *camellos* which provide a form of mass transport. A bus journey in Havana costs 40 centavos.

CAR & MOTORCYCLE HIRE

The two main car hire companies in Cuba are Transautos and Havanautos. They have offices at the airport and in and around the larger hotels in the main tourist centres. If you want to play it safe, book a fly/drive package through your travel agent. Car hire is not cheap, but it's by far the best option if you want to explore the country. Expect to pay about $60 per day and an additional $0.30 per km, plus insurance. If you plan to hire a car for a week or more, it's worth asking about all-inclusive rates. If you are paying in cash, you will be required to put down a deposit of around $200. A signed credit card slip is an accepted alternative. Horizontes Hoteles offer a combined hotel and hire car package deal known as the 'flexi fly and drive'.

On the Carretera Central linking Pinar del Río in the far west to Baracoa in the far east there are more than 40 petrol stations, most of them open 24 hours.

In tourist centres, such as Varadero, you can hire motorbikes for short excursions. Rates vary, between $3 to $5 for the first and $6 to $8 for the second hour.

CUSTOMS

Visitors may take a maximum of 20 kg of personal luggage into Cuba. You should expect to pay a heavy fine if this limit is exceeded. There is a limit of $250 on presents. Drugs, weapons and pornographic publications are strictly forbidden. Officially you may only export works of art which have been recorded in the register of Cuban assets; unofficially, a receipt is generally sufficient. The exportation of duty-free goods to EU countries is limited to: 200 cigarettes, 100 cigarillos, 50 cigars or 250 g of loose tobacco; 1 litre of rum over 22% proof or 2 litres less than 22% proof; 500 g coffee or 200 g coffee extracts; 50 g perfume or 0.25 l eau de toilette, plus gifts up to the value of $100. It is forbidden to import Cuban cigars into the USA. It is also illegal, under the CITES agreement, to take home any goods that may have been made from protected species.

DOMESTIC FLIGHTS

Long distances across Cuba can be covered quickly and cheaply on domestic flights operated by *Cubana de Aviación (Calle 23, no. 64, on the corner of Infanta, Vedado; Tel: 07/33 49 49 and 33 49 50)*. The planes are often quite old, few have more than 40 seats, and many of the flights get booked up well in advance. The flight network operates almost entirely out of Havana, with a limited number of direct links between the provincial airports of Baracoa, Camagüey, Cayo Largo, Ciego de Ávila, Cienfuegos, Isla de la Juventud, Manzanillo, Santiago de Cuba, Holguín, Sancti Spíritus, Santa Clara and Varadero. A single flight from Havana to Santiago de Cuba costs about $60. *Aerogaviota* operates flights from Havana to Camagüey, Holguín and Santiago de Cuba (*Havana office: Tel: 07/81 30 68*). Flights booked in advance should always be confirmed a day or two beforehand.

A company called *Aero-Taxi* charters private planes for excursions. The costs work out at about $20 for 12 minutes. *For further information: Havana, Calle 27, no. 102; Tel: 07/32 81 21 and 32 25 15/6.*

DRINKING WATER

To be on the safe side, it's advisable not to drink water from the tap, and to avoid fruit juices diluted with water.

DRIVING

The rules of the road here are pretty much the same as they are in Europe. Driving in Cuba is on the right, and remember that priority is given to traffic coming from the right on roundabouts. The main *autopistas* (motorways) are surprisingly smooth, and the traffic along them very light, though they are extremely badly signposted. Don't let the open road tempt you to put your foot down. Driving at high speed here can be very dangerous, and speed checks are regularly carried out. Police officers often lie in wait in concealed spots to pounce on drivers exceeding restrictions. The speed limit on motorways is 100 km/h (60 mph), 90 km/h (55 mph) on other roads, 50 km/h (30 mph) in built-up areas.

Cubans have an incredibly relaxed attitude to traffic, so always be on your guard for unexpected hazards. At motorway junctions, for example, you will often see crowds of people gathered round transporters, or fruit and vegetable stalls at the edge of the motorway. Traders will even wander out on to the carriageway to try and attract the custom of passing cars. Drive especially carefully along the country roads, where the majority of traffic is non-motorized, made up of people walking or cycling, riding on horseback or in carts. It's best to sound your horn when turning a blind bend, and when overtaking a large vehicle, as many of the old trucks do not have rear view mirrors.

When travelling through the countryside make sure you have a detailed map to hand which indicates exactly where the petrol stations are situated. Getting petrol is no longer a problem, but you should try to keep the tank half full as a precaution. There are a number of new, modern 'Servi' stations along the main roads, most of them open 24 hours a day. A litre of *especial* (four-star) costs around $1. It is illegal to carry a spare canister because of the risk of explosion in the heat.

EMBASSIES/CONSULATES

Britain
Cuban Consulate, 15 Grape St, London WC2H 8DR; Tel: 0171/ 240 2488

Cuban Embassy, 167 High Holborn, London WC1V 6PA; Tel: 0171/240 2488

Canada
Cuban Embassy, 388 Main St, Ottawa K1S 1E3; Tel: (613) 563 0141

Embassies in Cuba:
Britain
Calle 34, no. 708, between Calle 7 and 17, Miramar, Havana; Tel: 07/ 33 17 71 or 33 17 72 or 33 12 86 or 33 12 99 or 33 10 49 or 33 18 80

Canada
Calle 30, no. 518, between Calle 5 and 7, Miramar, Havana; Tel: 07/33 25 16 or 33 25 1 or 33 25 2 or 33 23 82 or 33 27 52

United States
United States Interests Section, Calzada, between L and M, Vedado, Havana; Tel: 07/33 35 43-47 or 33 35 51-59
From a traveller's point of view, this office has the same function as an embassy.

The shortage of medicines has taken its toll on the otherwise high standard of health care in Cuba, so you should always bring stocks of any vital medicines with you. Varadero has a modern, well-equipped clinic. In Havana, foreign visitors should contact the *Ciro García clinic (Calle 20, no. 4101, Marianao; Tel: 07/268 11)*. All holiday resorts have a *Clínica Internacional*. Doctors will visit you at your hotel for a fee of $30, and will do whatever is necessary in an emergency. You should take out an accident and illness insurance policy before leaving home.

The central information point for independent travellers in Cuba is the Office for Individual Tourism in the *Habana Libre Tryp* in Havana. Accommodation and all domestic flights can be booked here.
Calle L, on the corner of Calle 23 (Rampa), Vedado; Tel: 07/33 40 11, Fax: 33 31 41

Canada
Cuban Tourist Board, 55 Queen St East, Suite 705, Toronto, Ontario M5C 1R6; Tel: (416) 362 0700

United Kingdom
Cuban Tourist Office, 167 High Holborn, London WC1V 6PA; Tel: 0171/240 6655

United States
Center for Cuban Studies, 124 W 23rd St, New York, NY 10011; Tel: (212) 242-0559

For information in Cuba, contact:

Cubanacán
Corporación de Turismo y Comercio Internacional, S.A., Calle 23, between 15a and 17, Reparto Siboney, Ciudad de la Habana; Tel: 07/33 60 06, Fax: 07/33 60 46

Cubatur
Calle 23, no. 156, Vedado, Ciudad de la Habana; Tel: 07/33 41 55-60, Fax: 07/33 41 14

Horizontes Hoteles
S.A., Calle 23, no. 156, between Calle M and N, Vedado, Ciudad de la Habana; Tel: 07/33 40 42, Fax: 33 37 22

MARINAS

Yachts and motor boats have access to no less than nine marinas on the north coast and six on the south coast. As you enter Cuban waters, about 12 miles from the coast, you should either call the *Red Costera Nacional* on *HF* (*SSB*) *2760*, the *Red Turística* on *2790*, the *Autoridades Portuarias* on *VHF channel 68* or the *Turismo* on *channel 19*. The marinas on the north coast are in *Santa Lucía* (*Pinar del Río province*), *Havana, Varadero, Playa Santa Lucía* (*Camagüey province*), *Baracoa* and *Bahía de Naranjo* (*Holguín province*), all of which have harbours. The south coast marinas are in *Santiago de Cuba, Manzanillo, Ancón, Jagua, Cayo Largo* and the *Isla de la Juventud.* Yachts and small boats can be chartered at *Tarara Marina, Cayo Largo* and *Varadero.*

For information, contact: *Cadena de Marinas Puertosos, S. A., Ciudad de la Habana, Tel: 07/33 47 05, Fax: 33 47 03*

NEWSPAPERS

The official organ of the Cuban Communist Party is *Granma.* In hotels, it sells for $1, but officially costs just 20 centavos. The weekly digest, *Granma Internacional*, is perhaps of more interest to visitors as it contains adverts. *Viajeros especial Cuba*, published in Spanish and English, is a glossy magazine for tourists, usually given away free in five-star hotels. It contains some interesting articles and advice. Many magazines in English are available at newsstands in hotels and airports.

PASSPORTS & VISAS

Visitors are required to have a full passport and its expiry date must not fall within six months of your return date. Tourists are also required to have a Tourist Card (*tarjeta de turista*) which is valid for four weeks. If you are organizing your trip through a tour operator, then they will usually arrange this for you. If travelling independently, you should contact the Cuban embassy for an application form or (much quicker) go there in person, remembering to take your passport with you. The card costs £15 ($23). You can, as a last resort, get your tourist card at José Martí airport in Havana, though the process can be rather lengthy, and you will be at the mercy of local officials. If you are visiting Cuba on business or as a journalist, you must have both a special work permit and a visa.

PHOTOGRAPHY

Colour films are sold in most hotels and tourist shops, though they are relatively expensive. You can now take photos inside museums, though it's best to ask first as some charge for the privilege. Photographing military installations and factories is forbidden.

POST & TELEPHONES

Small post offices and telephone offices are located in the hotels and tourist areas (look out for signs marked *Teletel, EMS* or *DHL*). You can normally buy stamps, send faxes and make telephone calls from these booths. A telephone call to Europe costs an astronomical $6 per minute, and around $2.50 to Canada. To place an international call, dial 119, followed by the country code (UK: 44, Ireland: 353, US/Canada: 1), the area code (for numbers in Europe, omit the zero), and subscriber number. To make a call within Cuba, dial the area code (082 for Pinar del Río) and the local number. The international code for Cuba is 53.

Postcards and letters to Europe cost $0.50 and $0.80 respectively, and $0.40 and $0.70 to the Americas. They may well take several weeks to reach their destination.

TAXIS

The official tourist taxis congregate outside the big hotels, and have taximeters which calculate the fare in dollars. Travelling around town by taxi can be expensive. The journey from Vedado to the Ciudad Vieja (Havana old town), for example, costs about $6, while the fare from the airport to central Havana will be in the region of $20. On longer journeys the meter is switched off, so you will have to negotiate a price with the driver and make sure he has enough petrol to get you to your destination.

Alternatively, you can use the old American car taxis which gather at taxi stands and in central areas. These do not have meters and you should always establish a price beforehand.

You will need the help of the locals if you want to make use of the hard-to-identify *Panataxis*. They wait at most of the larger squares – but not outside hotels – and the drivers take payment in pesos, and usually carry several passengers at a time.

TIME ZONES

Cuba is five hours behind GMT and six hours behind Central European Time. From April to October, Cuba is on daylight-saving time (four hours behind GMT).

TIPPING

Cubans are always grateful for hard-currency tips. A normal tip for porters, and waiters and waitresses in hotel restaurants, would be $1, and about $3 per week for chambermaids. Tipping is not obligatory, but bear in mind that service charges are never included in restaurant bills.

TRAINS

Santiago de Cuba, Cienfuegos and Pinar del Río are linked by rail, but the service is not very reliable. Tickets are available in Havana from *Ferrotour* (*Arsenal y Egido; Tel: 07/62 17 70*). If you want to book two adjacent seats, make sure you stipulate this at the time of booking. The 16-hour journey from Havana to Santiago costs about $35.

TV & RADIO

Aside from the state-run channels, the televisions in the larger hotels broadcast CNN and other foreign channels, which are received via satellite. The official radio station broadcasts Radio Rebelde; a newcomer to the air is the lively commercial station, Radio Ritmo.

WHEN TO GO

The sun shines in Cuba all year round, but to avoid high humid-ity levels, it's best to travel in the dry season (Nov-April). The north-east wind during this period is also much more gentle. The riskiest period for hurricanes is between the end of August and the beginning of October. The wet season falls between June and October. Though the rainfall is heavy, the showers are short.

Electrical appliances usually run on 110V 60 Hz, but most European joint venture hotels have a 220V mains network and sockets take the American flat pin plugs. It is always advisable to ask at the reception about the power supply and to carry an adaptor.

WEATHER IN HAVANA
Seasonal averages

Daytime temperatures in °C/F

Jan	Feb	Mar	Apr	May	Jun	Jul	Aug	Sept	Oct	Nov	Dec
26/79	27/81	28/82	29/84	30/86	31/88	31/88	32/90	31/88	29/84	27/81	26/79

Night-time temperatures in °C/F

Jan	Feb	Mar	Apr	May	Jun	Jul	Aug	Sept	Oct	Nov	Dec
18/64	18/64	19/66	21/70	22/72	23/73	24/75	24/75	24/75	23/73	21/70	19/66

Sunshine: hours per day

Jan	Feb	Mar	Apr	May	Jun	Jul	Aug	Sept	Oct	Nov	Dec
6	6	7	7	8	6	6	6	5	5	5	5

Rainfall: days per month

Jan	Feb	Mar	Apr	May	Jun	Jul	Aug	Sept	Oct	Nov	Dec
6	4	4	4	7	10	9	10	11	11	7	6

Sea temperatures in °C/F

Jan	Feb	Mar	Apr	May	Jun	Jul	Aug	Sept	Oct	Nov	Dec
25/77	24/75	24/75	26/79	27/81	27/81	28/82	28/82	28/82	28/82	27/81	27/81

Do's and don'ts

*How to avoid some of the pitfalls
that face the unwary traveller*

Street hassle

Hawkers and hustlers congregate in the main city centres and mill around tourists like bees around a honey pot. You will be offered all sorts of goods and services, from bad quality cigars to women companions. While this constant pestering can be annoying it is rarely aggressive and a polite, but firm, refusal is usually enough to get the message across. That said, some of the services offered can be useful. For a small consideration, you can get help finding a private room or a private restaurant, or even get yourself a guide to show you around the town.

Crime and begging

The crime rate on Cuba is still relatively low, being confined mainly to pickpocketing and petty theft. Although the government is trying to stop the situation from getting any worse by threatening drastic penalties, there is no guarantee that this policy will work. Begging is a recent phenomenon, the inevitable result of burgeoning tourism. The majority of beggars are children, who hang around in

groups and pester tourists mercilessly. Giving children money does nothing but upset the social balance; biros or chewing gum perhaps, but only in moderation as these items will simply be sold on like any other commodity. If children find they can make money easily from tourists, this will undermine the work ethic, prevent the development of an ordered society and increase crime. The authorities are trying hard to stop the situation from worsening, and responsible tourists should do their best to help them by discouraging begging themselves.

The importance of tact

The best way to get by in Latin American countries is to adopt an open and friendly approach to the local people. A brief conversation with hotel staff who may have been trained in some basic English, or a few words in Spanish, if you feel confident enough, with the locals you meet while travelling, helps to bridge the cultural gap. Avoid making direct, critical remarks as this can cause offence. Latin Americans prefer to couch unfavourable comments in polite, but evasive terms. That does not mean you have to ignore careless incidents and smile graciously through thick and thin, as that can be interpreted as a sign of weakness and work equally to your disadvantage. In awkward situations – poor service in an overpriced restaurant for example – it is advisable to voice your complaint firmly but politely. Speaking angrily to someone will be taken as a personal insult and will get you nowhere.

Machismo

A woman walking unaccompanied on the streets of Cuba rarely goes by unnoticed. Cuban men, like all Latinos, are masters of the throwaway chat-up line. They will stare at and often follow an attractive woman, hissing or whispering compliments to her, anything from *reina* (queen) and *belleza* (beauty) to more vulgar suggestions. The comments are generally addressed to women on the move, which means they can be easily ignored. These approaches are pretty harmless, and it would be pointless to take offence or get angry, unless of course they get out of hand, which they rarely do. Cuba is still one of the safest countries in Latin America and violent crime against women is almost unheard of. Macho behaviour is innate in this part of the world, and is just part of the game that Latin American men simply have to play.

Another type of harassment comes from young men who try to befriend female visitors in the hope of gaining access to tourist haunts and picking up a few dollars. These offers are best ignored.

Topless bathing

There may have been a social revolution on Cuba, but the sexual revolution that changed attitudes in Europe and America in the 1960s did not happen here. Going topless or wearing very brief bikinis is as frowned upon here as it is in Mexico, Venezuela, Colombia, Brazil, or any other Catholic country in Latin America. Cuban men will go into paroxysms of delight at the sight of young tourists in skimpy beachwear, but topless bathing is regarded as provocative exhibitionism, besides which it is illegal. Obscene literature and photos are not tolerated on Cuba, but the advent of tourism and the growth of prostitution has led to a relaxation in attitudes.

Drugs

Although it is widely known that Cuba has in the past aided and abetted Colombian drug barons on the pretext that this would harm the USA, there is no drug trade on the island. Drugs are strictly forbidden. The Cuban authorities use trained sniffer dogs, and anyone found in possession of any type of drug will quickly discover what life is like inside a Cuban jail.

Prostitution

Sadly, prostitution is on the rapid increase, encouraged by the increasing number of unscrupulous western men who shower young Cuban girls with gifts and dollars in return for sexual favours. Unaccompanied male tourists wandering through Havana should expect to have to brush off pimps offering them the companionship of young Cuban girls.

Road Atlas of Cuba

Please refer to back cover for an overview of this road atlas

Golfo de México

Archipiélago

Oj

Punta Tabaco

Cayo Diego

Macurije

44

Ensenada de Dimas

Dimas

Cayo Rapado Grande

NACION

La Ceja de Izquierdo

30

Santa María

Santa Isabel

Mina

Cayos de Buenavista

Arroyos de Mantua

Pino Gordo

Sierra

La Vigía

13

Mantua

La Pimienta

San Felipe

C

El Blanquizal

San

del

Juan Gómez

Cayo Zapato

El Ají

35

Veinte de Mayo

10

Golfo de Guanahacabibes

Bolívar

Jos

Punta Pinalillo

Salado

12

San Ju

Punta Colorada

Bahía

Embalse Laguna Grande

Sandino

Punta Plumajes

Le Fe

15

Lag

Alca

Punta la Majagua

Ensenada Melones

11

Las

Punta Carabela Grande

Guanahacabibes

Los Insinitos

El Cayuco

Martina

Carabelita

La Jaula

La Jarreta

32

Pasa Sorda del Muerto

Punta Cajón

Cayos de la Leña

de

PARQUE NACIONAL

33

Vallecito

La Güira

Cabo de Yucatán

Punta Gorda

La Bajada

Valle San Juan

Yayales

Cabo de San Antonio

Ensenada Cajón

Península

Bolondrón

Los Ingleses

DE PENÍNSULA DE

Cueva Funche

Los Cayuelos

GUANAHACABIBES

Bahía de Corrientes

Uvero Quemado

Estrecho de Yucatán

Punta del Holandés

Punta Caimán

María la Gorda

Cabo Corrientes

Punta Leones

A

Estrecho de

Ciudad de La Hab

★★ **LA HABANA**

Punta Campanilla ★ Playa
Cojimar
Barreras
★ Museo Históri
de CristóbaCo

SANTA
FE
Playa
Baracoa Cangrejeras **El Cano**
39 **Punta**
Mosquito **Habana** **Brava** Walay **Santiago de**
La Boca **Libre** **Bauta** Guatao **las Vegas**
Bahía a La Habana **Mariel** Corralillo **El** Cu.
Punta **Agusto César** **Caimito** **Rincón** C.
Playa **los Ciegos** **Sandino** Mi **Managu**
San Pedro **49** Guayabal **Rancho** Bejucal **48**
Pablo D.I. **Cabanas** **Quiebra Hacha** **Vereda** Volcán S
Torriente **Guanajay** **Ciba del** **Nueva** La Río11 de
Brau Valdés 408 **Agua** **San Antonio** **Salud** Hondo 10 **San A**
San Juan Loma del Rubi 15 **Eduardo García** **de los Baños** **Quivicán** **San** de las
de Dios El Guzço **Cayajabos** **Lavandero** 13 **Felipe** **Guara**
Valdés **Artemisa** **Capellania** Las **El**
ono's Mango **Loma la Caoba** 534 **Abraham** **Canas** **Gabriel** San **Meler**
Bonito 635 Soroa 17 **Lincoln** **Alquizar** El **Güira de** **Camacho** Serafina **del**
San 12 **Pijirigua** **Neptuno** Rosano **El Junco Melena** 9 San 15
Cristóbal **Candelaria** 18 **Las** 32 **Guanímar** **Agustín**
ngo **Mango** **183** **Mangas** Ojo de **Batabai**
Jobo **Dulce** 6 Playa Agua **Playa**
Los Pinos **El Corojal** Majana Playa Punta **del Cajío** **Surgidero**
o Taco **José Martí** Ensenada Guanímar de Cayamas **de Batabanó**
208 Fajardo Salina de Majana
Piedra Corojal Cayería
Cantón Punta Cayos los Cayamas
Trujillo **El Pinar** de las Salinas los Guzmanes **La** **Ha**
Sur Punta Punta
Laguna Comegatos la Capitana Canal del Hacha
de la Deseada Cayo
Ensenada **G o l f o** **d e** Buenavista
de Bacunagua Cayo
Mail Punta Guis
una País Punta Gor
dia Casa **B a t a b a n ó** Cayo Mataram
guao Canal de la Laguna Cayo Culebra Monterrey Ma
Cayo
Rabihorcado Punta
2 h
Cayo
Cuarto
Canal de la Pipa

Islas de Mangles
Cayos Alacranes
Cayos la Monteca
Cayo
Punta Grande **A r c h i p i é**
Punta
Punta del la Bibijagua
del Lindero Chacón 102
104 a
261 ★ Presidio Cayo el Navío
Modelo la Cruz

Numbers/Grid labels
1, 2, 3, 4, 5, 6 (left margin)
A, B, C (top)

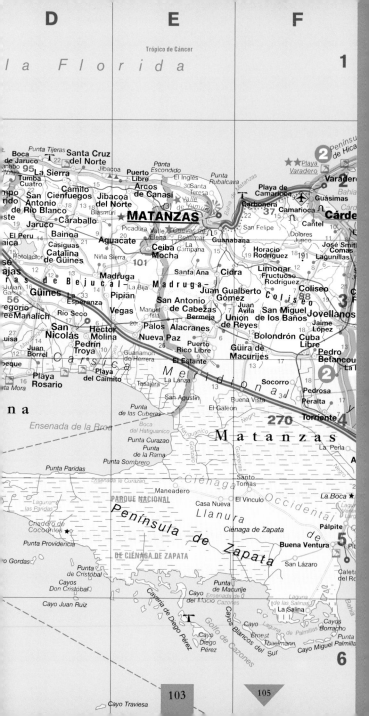

Trópico de Cáncer

la F l o r i d a

Punta Tijeras Santa Cruz del Norte
Boca de Jaruco
anabó **95** La Sierra
Tumba Cuatro
Camilo Jibacoa
San Cienfuegos del Norte
Antonio de Río Blanco
Cáraballo
El Perú Bainoa
aica Casiguas
Catalina Niña Sierra
de Güines
ajas
Madruga La Bija
Güines La Esperanza
egorio Río Seco Vegas
eeMañalich
San Héctor
Nicolás Molina Palos
Juan Pedrín Troya Nueva Paz
Borrel
beque Carsica
Playa Playa
Rosario del Caimito Tasajera
ta Mora

Jibacoa
Puerto Libre El Inglés
Arcos de Canasí 30 Santa Teresa
Picadura Valle de Yumurí
MATANZAS
Aguacate Valle Elena
Ceiba La Campana
Mocha Guanábana
Santa Ana Cidra
Madruga– Juan Gualberto
Gómez
San Antonio Juan
de Cabezas Ávila
Bermeja Unión de Reyes
Alacranes San
Puerto Güira de
Rico Libre Macurijes
El Estante
La Lanza Meridional
San Agustín Buena Vista
El Galeón

Punta Escondido
Punta Rubalcava
Playa de Camarioca
Carbonera 37
San Felipe Camarioca
Dolores Junco
Horacio 19 Rodríguez
Limonar 12 Fructuoso Rodríguez
Coliseo 58
San Miguel
de los Baños Jovellanos
Bolondrón Cuba Libre
Pedro Betancour
Socorro Pedrosa
Peralta 17
Torriente

Península de Hica
★★ Playa Varadero
Varadero
Guásimas
Camarioca Cárde
Cantel
José Smith Comas
Lagunillas
Coliseo
Jaime López
La

Ensenada de la Broa

n a

Boca del Hatiguanico
Punta Curazao
Punta de la Rama
Punta Sombrero

Punta Paridas

Ensenada le Curazao

Laguna las Paridas

Criadero de Cocodrilos ★

Punta Providencia

ro Gordas

Punta de Cristóbal
Cayos Don Cristóbal

Cayo Juan Ruiz

Maneadero

PARQUE NACIONAL

Casa Nueva
El Vínculo
Santo Tomás

Ciénaga Occidental

Península de Zapata

DE CIÉNAGA DE ZAPATA

Llanura

Ciénaga de Zapata

San Lázaro

Punta de Macurije Cayo del Macío
Golfo de Cazones
Cayo Diego Pérez
Cayos Blancos del Sur

La Boca ★
Pálpite
Buena Ventura 5
Caleta del Ro
La Salina
Cayos Borracho
Cayo Miguel Palmilla

Cayo Traviesa

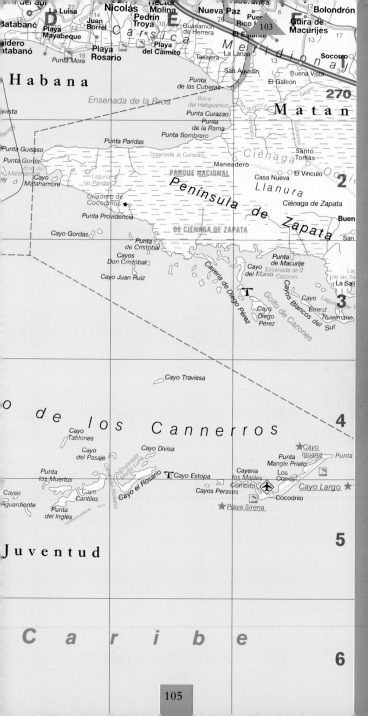

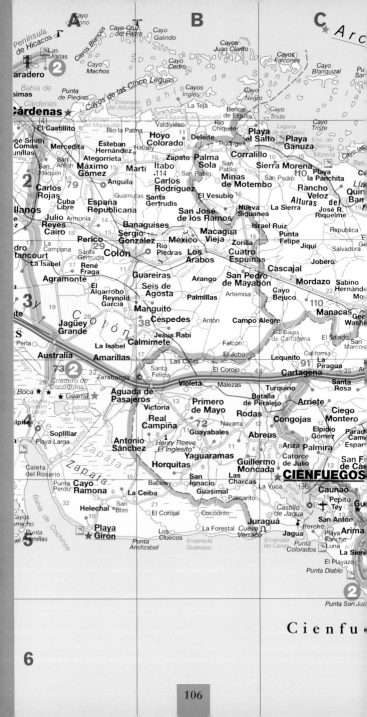

1

2

3

4

5

6

Verde

Boca de Cueva
Cayo Esquivel
Sotavento del Sur
Cayo del Cristo

Puerto
Cayo
Bomba
Grande
Punta
Gorda

V i l l a   C l a r a

Cayo
Dromedarias

Cayo
Lanzanillo

C a n a l   d e

S a n   N i c o l á s

San

de

Los Tubos
Isabela
de Sagua
Bahía de
Úbero
San Jorge
aguaguas
El Mogote
Playa
Úbero
Norte
Cayo la Vaca
Playa Piñón
Cayo Vaca
Enseñada de
Cayos del
Pajonal
Cayo
Marcos

de

S a b a n a

Armonía
Punta
Trujillo
Bocas de Marcos
Punta
Higuereta
Cayo Fragoso

mado
güines
181
Sagua
la Grande
Granadillo
Emilio
Córdova
Playa
Juan Francisco

Viana

Sitiecito
ranes
Mariana
Grajales
28
53
6
Unidad
Proletaria
24
Perucho
Figueredo
las
El Santo
Cayo Guayo
Cayos de la Vinzón
Cay

Amaro
Cifuentes
El
Vaquerito
16
Calabazar de
Sagua
Arroyo
Naranjo
25
Villas
Camacho
Punta Gorda
Cayo
Guayo
B a h í a

nto
omingo
intiseis
e Julio
Mata
San
Francisco
Encrucijada
Chiquí Gómez
30
San Diego
del Valle
Sin Nombre
San Miguel
Vega Alta
La Luz
19
Refugio
San Antonio
de las Vueltas
Jinaguayabo
Marcelo
Salado
Caibarién

otea
Nombre de Dios
Hatillo
Yabú
Palenque
Cayo
Aguado

Esperanza
Antón
Díaz
16
El
Gigante
27
53
Camajuaní
Taguayabón
Remedios
Guani
Boca del Robalo

huelo
Castaño
José María
Pérez
Bartolomé
Zulueta
Dólores
35

Efraín
Alfonso
es
12
**SANTA
CLARA**
22
(200)
Manajanabo
Falcón
14
Zulueta
del Sur
Heriberto
Duquesne
Seibabo
Buena
Vista
Juan
Francisco
Obo
Mo

a Ramona
San Juan
de los Yeras
Carretera del
Acueducto
Miller
Alturas
Placetas
El Copey
Hermanos
Ameijeiras
El Mamey
Yagu

rillo
Jorobada
Oropesa
Aguas
Blancas
Benito
Juárez
84
Remates
Carrillo
General
Menes

El Tejón
Biajaca
Matagua
396
Báez
390
Santa
Las Pozas
26
Manzanares
Jarahueca
Minas
Abajo
Centro
Comuna
Manuel M

Barajagua
Presa
Avilés
348
La
Moza
María Rodríguez
11
Los Indios
Nazareno
Dío de
Agua
Potrerillo

anayagua
co
Manicaragua
Agabama
La Redonda
Neiva
La Ra

scas
Presa
Hanabanilla
Hanabanilla
El Salte del
Hanabanilla
Mina
San Antonio
Fomento
Mabujina
Santa
Lucía
Guayos
Cabaiguán
32
La Amist

citas
Pico
San Juan
1140
El Nicho
Jibacoa
Güinía
de Miranda
Santa
Rosa
Embalse de
Tuinicú
Las
Cuabas
Tuinicú
**Zaza
del Medio**
Sigüan

Mayarí
806
Topes de
Collantes
PAISAJE NATURAL
La Felicidad
Sopimpa
El
Mamoncillo
Aeropuerto

ilo
999
Topes
de Collantes
PROTEGIDO
Casa
de Tablas
753
Loma la Gloria
Las Tosas
**Sancti
Spíritus**
Serg
Gonz

iegos
COLLANTES
931
Macizo
de
Meyer
G u a m u h a y a

Valle de
Yaguanabo
Río Hondo
Pico de
Potrerillo
Valle de los
Ingenios
Condado
Loma de Banco
842
22
Presa
Pe

Piti Fajardo
Magua
Iznaga
Caracusey
Banao
San
Antonio
Zaza
Ferrola

79
La Boca
Trinidad
Torre de Iznaga
La Pedrera
70
Paredes

Playa Ancón
Casilda
Cuyují
(20)
Palmarito
La Güira
Pojabo
Guasimal
Cayo Yero

Península
de Ancón
El Caracol
San Pedro
Vallejo
Heriberto
Orellanes
Pera

Punta Manatí
Bahía
Playa
Tayabacoa
Cagueira
Tunas
de Zaza
Siete de
Noviembre
Mapos

107

de Ciego
Santa
Ciego
El Mámu
Rome

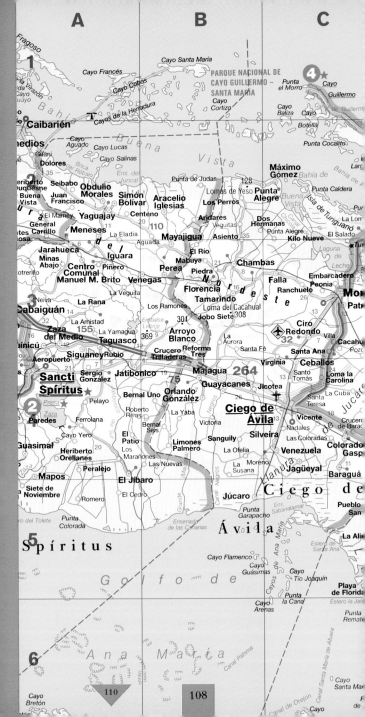

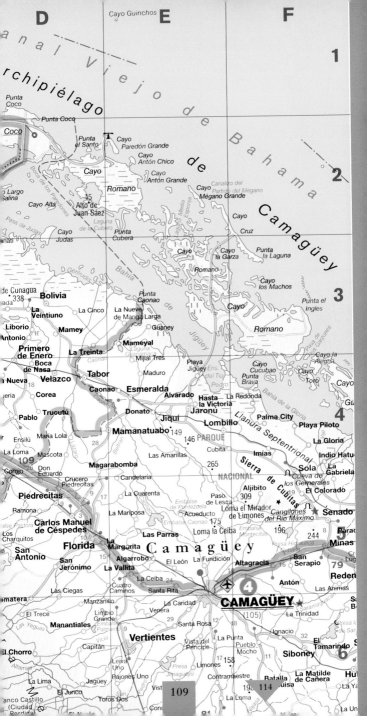

D **E** **F**

Cayo Guinchos

1

C a n a l   V i e j o   d e   B a h a m a

Punta
Coco

A r c h i p i é l a g o

Punta Coco

Coco

Punta
el Santo

Cayo
Paredón Grande

Cayo
Antón Chico

2

Boca de los Paredones

Cayo
Romano

Cayo
Antón Grande

Canalizo del
Partín del Mégano

o Largo
Salina

45
Alto de
Juan Sáez

Cayo
Mégano Grande

d e   C a m a g ü e y

Cayo Alta

Pasa de Judas

Laguna
de la Cubera

Cayo
Cruz

anati

Cayo
Judas

Punta
Cubera

Laguna Media Espinosa

Cayo

Cayo
la Garza

Cayo
la Laguna

Punta
la Laguna

Bahía

Romano

Cayo
los Machos

Jiguey

3

de Cunagua
ada 338

Bolivia

La Cinco

Punta
Caonao

de

Cayo

Punta el
Ingles

Liborio
Antonio

**La
Veintiuno**

La Nueve
de Manga Larga

Guáney

Romano

Pasa de Carrones

Mamey

**Primero
de Enero**

La Treinta

Mameyal

Laguna
Guacamara

Mijial Tres

Playa
Jiguey

Ens.
del Tio
Pedro

Cayo
Cucubao
Punta
Brava

Cayo la
Alegría

Nueva

**Boca
de Nasa**

Velazco

Tabor

Maduro

Cayo
Toro

Cayo

jería

Corea

Caonao

Esmeralda

Alvarado

**Hasta
la Victoria**

La Redonda

Bahía de la Gloria

Gu

4

Pablo

Trucutú

María Lola

Donato

Jiquí

Jaronu

Palma City

Playa Piloto

Ensilú

28

Mamanatuabo 149

Lombillo

La Loma

109

Mascota

Batrón

146 **PARQUE**

Cubita

Imias

**La
Gloria**

Indio Hatu

Corojo

**Don
Eduardo**

Magarabomba

Las Amarillas

265

Sierra

Sola

**La
Gabriela**

Cueva de
los Gemerales

Piedrecitas

Crucero
Piedrecitas

9

Candelaria

La Cuarenta

17

NACIONAL

Aljibito
309

Paso
de Lesca

de Cubitas

El Colorado

Ramona

3

alse Pastora

Los
Charquitos

**Carlos Manuel
de Céspedes**

**San
Antonio**

Florida

**La
Margarita**

La Mariposa

Embalse de Puntezuela

Acueducto

Embalse Caonao 175

Las Parras

Loma el Mirador
de Limones

Loma la Ceiba

Cangilones
del Río Máximo

Embalse
Montecitas

196

Senado

244

8

Para

Minas

79

**San
Jerónimo**

Algarrobo

La Vallita

El León

La Fundición

C a m a g ü e y

Altagracia

16

**San
Serapio**

Reden

La Ceiba

24

Cuatro
Caminos

Las Ciegas

Manzanillo

Santa Rita

Antón

Las Animas

CAMAGÜEY

La Trinidad

Sa
B

amatera

El Trece

Limpio
Grande

Venera

La Caridad

(105)

La

Manantiales

Embalse
Palmira

9

Santa Rosa

12

Ignacio

32

**El
Tamarindo**

S

6

El Chorro

Capitán

Vicio

Vertientes

Vista del
Príncipe

La Punta

Pueblo
Mocho

11

Siboney

La Lima

Leiva
Uno

Jagüey

Pajones Uno

Presa
Jimaguayú

Limones

17 158

Contramaestre

Hu

Altamira

El Junco

Toros Dos

Vist

109

190 114

**Batalla
Luisa**

**La Matilde
de Cañera**

La Ya

anco Castillo
(Ciudad
Perdida)

Cond

La Loma

La Un

Sancti   Spíritus

Golfo   de

Ana   María

Archipiélago   de   los   Jardines

Laberinto   de   las   Doce   Leguas

(Jardir

Mar
Caribe

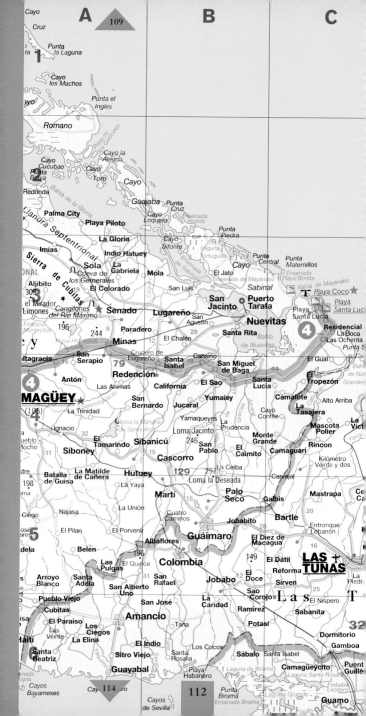

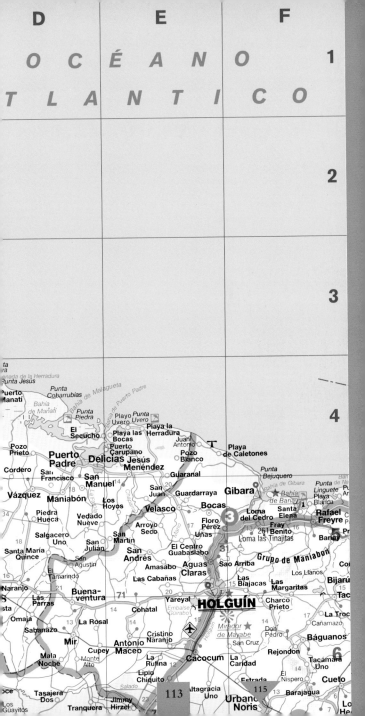

D

Pozo
Prieto

Puerto
Padre

ordero
San
Francisco

ázquez
Maniabón

Piedra
Hueca

anta María
Quince

Salgacero
Uno

San
Julián

aranjo
El
Tamarindo

Las
Parras

Buena-
ventura

71

Omaja
Sabanazo

La Rosal

Mir

Mala
Noche

Monte
Alto

Cupey

Tasajera
Dos

ayitos
Tranquera

Cauto
Embarcadero
Cauto

Guasimilla

ra

del Cauto
Las
Mangas

E

Bocas
Puerto
Carupano

Delicias Jesús
Menéndez

San
Manuel

Los
Hoyos

Vedado
Nueve

San
Martin

San
Andrés

Amasabo

Las Cabañas

Juan
Antonio

Pozo
Blanco

Guaranal

San
Juan

Guardarraya

Velasco

Arroyo
Seco

Floro
Pérez

El Centro
Guabasiabo

Aguas
Claras

Yareyal

Cohatal

Antonio
Maceo

La
Rufina

Lipio
Chiquito

Cristino
Naranjo

Cacocum

Playa
de Caletones

Gibara

Loma
del Cedro

Uñas

Sao Arriba

Las
Biajacas

Charco
Prieto

Embalse
Guirabo

HOLGUÍN

Holguín

Mirador
de Mayabe

San Cruz

La
Caridad

Salado

Altagracia
Uno

La
Julia

Urbano
Noris

Jimmy
Hirzel

71

Cauto
Cristo

Cautillo
Abajo

Babiney

Cauto Guacanayabo

Cauto
la Yaya

Papi
Lastre

El Coco

Algodones
Dos

Dos Rios

Embalse
las Villas

Mije
Hueco

Estrada

El
Nispero

Barajagua

Calera

Flora

Parana

Lora

Santa
Elena

El
Caserio

Ya
Veremos

F

Punta
Bejuquero

Bahía de Gibara

Bahía
de Bariay

Santa
Elena

Fray
Benito

Loma las Tinajitas

Grupo de Maniabon

Los Llanos

Las
Margaritas

Don
Pedro

Rejondon

Tacámara
Uno

Cueto

Punta
Lingueta

Rafael
Freyre

Bariay

Bijarú

La Troch

Cañamazo

Báguanos

Cor

Tac

Lo
Hed

Alto

Mango
Barag

Palmarito
de Cauto

Mabay

Barranca

El Dátil

Corojito

Nuevo
Yao

Buey
Arriba

San Pablo

PARQUE
NACIONAL DE
TURQUINO

Pico
Bayamesa
1974

Pico Real del
Turquino

1730

as Ocujal

Ensenada
de las Mulas

BAYAMO

Santa
Rita

Horno
Guisa

La Teodora

Santa
Bárbara

Los
Horneros

Jiguaní

76

Charco
Redondo

Los
Negros

Victorino Matias
1287

El Franco
Arriba

788

M

El
Cadillo

1128
Loma el Jobo

Uvero

Balre

Maffo

Contramaestre

América

Aguacate

Ramón
de Cuaninao

Cruz de
los Baños

La
Colorada

Embalse Carlos Manuel
de Céspedes

Palma
Soriano

Presa Gilbert

Dos
Palmas

La
Marsellesa

43

Dos
Rios

El Te

Ballaire

S Me

Pico Bayamesa

Cabagan

Chivirico

Bayamita

Punta
Bayamita

Punta
Tabacal

Las
Coloradas

PARQUE
NACIONAL

El Cobre

Caletón
Blanco

30

del

5

Boca de Cab

S a n t i a g o   d e

Bahía de Santiago

6

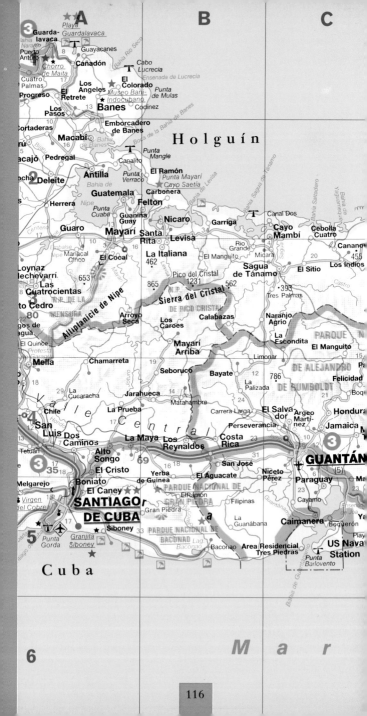

This map shows an area of Cuba including the provinces of Holguín, Santiago de Cuba, and Guantánamo.

A

Playa Guardalavaca
Guarda-lavaca
Bahía Naranjo
Puerto Antonio
Guayacanes
Chorro de Maita
Cuatro Palmas
Cañadón
Progreso
Los Angeles
El Retrete
Cabo Lucrecia
Ensenada de Lucrecia
El Colorado
Museo Baní-Indocubano
Punta de Mulas
Codinez
Banes
Los Pasos
Cortaderas
Embórcadero de Banes
Macabí
Bahía de Banes
Boca de la Bahía de Banes
acajó
Pedregal
Punta Mangle
Canalito
ocha
Deleite
Antilla
Punta Verraco
El Ramón
Punta Mayarí
Cayo Saetía
Herrera
Nipe
Bahía de
Guatemala
Carbonera
Guanina Guay
Felton
Punta Cuaba
Guaro
Mayarí
Santa Rita
Nicaro
Levisa
Garriga
Canal Dos
Cayo Mambí
Cebolla Cuatro

Holguín

B

C

Bahía Río Seco
Bahía de Levisa
Sagua du Levisa
Bahía Sagua de Tánamo
Bahía Sabinal

Loynaz
lechevarrí
Las Cuatrocientas
to Cedro
gos de
agua
El Quince
Protesta
Mella
Chamarreta
Embalse
Nipe
Manacal Cinco
El Cocal
La Italiana
462
El Manguito
Pico del Cristal
1231
865
N.P.
DE RICO CRISTAL
Sierra del Cristal
562
Rio Grande
Midara
Sagua de Tánamo
El Sitio
Canano
455
Los Indios
393
Tres Palmas
Naranjo Agrio
La Escondita
El Manguito
Limonar
Altuplanicie de Nipe
Arroyo Seca
Los Caroes
Calabazas
Mayarí Arriba
Seboruco
Bayate
La Palizada
786
Felicidad
Boq
Castro
PARQUE N
DE ALEJANDRO
DE HUMBOLDT

Chile
La Cucaracha
Jarahueca
La Prueba
Matahambre
Carrera Larga
El Salvador
Argeo Martínez
Honduras
Jamaica
San Luis
Dos Caminos
La Maya
Los Reynaldos
Costa Rica
Perseverancia
Tetuán
Alto Songo
San José
GUANTÁN
Melgarejo
El Cristo
Boniato
El Caney
Yerba de Guinea
El Aguacate
Niceto Pérez
Paraguay
(5)
Ma
Virgen del Cobre
SANTIAGO
DE CUBA
Gran Piedra
PARQUE NACIONAL DE GRAN PIEDRA
Filipinas
Cayamo
Caimanera
Boquerón
Ya
Punta Gorda
Granjita Siboney
Siboney
PARQUE NACIONAL DE BACONAD
Baconao
La Guanábana
Area Residencial Tres Piedras
Punta Barlovento
US Nava Station
Play

Cuba

M a r

D   **E**   **F**

O C É A N O   **1**

T L A N T I C O

2

Cayo
Moa Grande
Bahía Yaguasey
Punta Gorda
Abajo   Punta
     Guarico
rrey   Quemado   *Bahía de Cañete*
  del Negro   **Yamanigüey**
         Punta
illas de Moa   Santa María   del Mangle
           Punta
1175   La Vega   Barlovento
ico del Toldo   de Taco   Morel
    Arroyo Bueno   709   Maguana   **3**
e Sagua   **Cayo Güin**
    921   676   Yunque   *Boca*
     de Baracoa ★   *del Toa*
Arroyo   **Paso de Toa**
el Medio Pico Galán   Punta   Punta
Bernardo   ·974   ★ **Baracoa**   Rama   del Fraile
oro   *Baracoa*   Fortaleza
           ③   ⊹Matachín   **Sabana**
     Puriales   712   Los Hoyos   *Viaducto La Farola*   ⊤ Punta
   de Caujerí   **Jamal**   **Maisí**   de Maisí
        Sabanilla   **Mosquitero**   Los   Punta
            Cagüeybaje   Panchos   de Quema⊤
        Sierra del Purial   **Capiro**
Guaibanó   Pico el Gato   603   La Cuchilla   **La Maquina**
·747   1176   *La Farola*   **Los**
  Mariana   27   La Tinta   **Llanos** ⊤
San Antonio   133   **Imías**
del Sur   20   15   **Cajobabo**   Punta Negra
quirí   Macambo   Punta   Jauco   *Punta Caleta*
   24   Imías
Tortuguilla   **4**

Sierra de Mariana

Bahía de Baracoa
Bahía Sabanalamar
Bahía de Imías
Bahía de Baitiquirí

Punta del Fraile

Bahía de Ovando

Paso de los Vientos

u a n t á n a m o   **5**

C a r i b e   **6**

117

ROAD ATLAS LEGEND

Autobahn mit Anschlußstelle
Motorway with junction

Autobahn in Bau
Motorway under construction

Autobahn in Planung
Motorway projected

Autobahnähnliche Schnell-
straße mit Anschlußstelle
Dual carriage-way with
motorway characteristics
with junction

Straße mit zwei
getrennten Fahrbahnen
Dual carriage-way

Durchgangsstraße
Thoroughfare

Wichtige Hauptstraße
Important main road

Hauptstraße
Main road

Sonstige Straße
Other road

Fahrweg
Carriageway

Straßen in Bau
Roads under construction

Eisenbahn
Railway

Autofähre
Car ferry

Schiffahrtslinie
Shipping route

Landschaftlich besonders
schöne Strecke
Route with
beautiful scenery

Straße gegen Gebühr befahrbar
Toll road

1357 Paß mit Höhenangabe
Pass with height

Bedeutende Steigungen
Important gradients

Salzsee
Saltwater lake

Sumpf
Swamp

Salzsumpf
Saltwater swamp

Mangrove
Mangrove

Korallenriff
Coral reef

Kultur
Culture

★★ **PARIS**
★★ *la Alhambra*   Eine Reise wert
Worth a journey

★ **TRENTO**
★ *Comburg*   Lohnt eine Umweg
Worth a detour

Landschaft
Landscape

★★ **Rodos**
★★ *Fingal's cave*   Eine Reise wert
Worth a journey

★ **Korab**
★ *Jaskinia raj*   Lohnt einen Umweg
Worth a detour

Besonders schöner Ausblick
Important panoramic view

PARQUE NACIONAL   Nationalpark, Naturpark
National park, nature park

4807   Bergspitze mit Höhenangabe
in Metern
Mountain summit with height
in metres

(630)   Ortshöhe
Height above sea level

Kirche
Church

Kirchenruine
Church ruin

Turm
Tower

Leuchtturm
Lighthouse

Schloß, Burg
Palace, castle

Schloß-, Burgruine
Palace ruin, castle ruin

Denkmal
Monument

Wasserfall
Waterfall

Höhle
Cave

Ruinenstätte
Ruins

★ Sonstiges Objekt
Other object

Campingplatz
Camp site

Badestrand · Surfen
Bathing beach · Surfing

Tauchen · Fischen
Diving · Fishing

Verkehrsflughafen
Airport

Flugplatz
Airfield

20 km
10mi